UNIVERSITY OF NOTRE DAME

LITURGICAL STUDIES

VOLUME IX

Liturgical Studies

DEPARTMENT OF THEOLOGY OF THE
UNIVERSITY OF NOTRE DAME

Liturgical Piety
REV. LOUIS BOUYER (OF THE ORATORY)

Church Buildings and Furnishings
REV. J. B. O'CONNELL

The Bible and the Liturgy
REV. JEAN DANIELOU, S.J.

Worship: The Life of the Missions
REV. JOHANNES HOFINGER, S.J.

The Meaning of Sacred Scripture
REV. LOUIS BOUYER (OF THE ORATORY)

The Early Liturgy
REV. JOSEF A. JUNGMANN, S.J.

Rite and Man:
Natural Sacredness and Christian Liturgy
REV. LOUIS BOUYER (OF THE ORATORY)

Proclaiming God's Message:
A Study in the Theology of Preaching
REV. DOMENICO GRASSO, S.J.

Realization
Anthropology and Pastoral Care
JOSEF GOLDBRUNNER

REALIZATION
Anthropology of Pastoral Care

Liturgical Studies

REALIZATION

Anthropology of Pastoral Care

BY

JOSEF GOLDBRUNNER

Translated by Paul C. Bailey, C.S.C.
and
Elisabeth Reinecke

UNIVERSITY OF NOTRE DAME PRESS
1966

Imprimi Potest: Howard J. Kenna, C.S.C., *Provincial*

Nihil Obstat: Joseph Hoffman, C.S.C., *Censor Deputatus*

Imprimatur: ✠ Leo A. Pursley, D.D., L.L.D.,
Bishop of Fort Wayne-South Bend
April 30, 1966

Library of Congress Catalog Card Number 66-14629

Contents

vii

Foreword

REALIZATION means the actualization of faith—a faith fully awakened and effective within man. This is a meeting of seed and soil, of God and human nature, an encounter between the divine Person and the human person at the point where theology and anthropology touch each other. The main emphasis of this book is, therefore, anthropological, since this area is the primary concern of priests and educators, whose task it is not only to sow the Word of God but also to prepare the soil for it. And since the conditioning of the soil requires considerably more care than does the sowing of the seed, our reflections— the fruit of decades of striving to bring science and practical experience together—are focused on a doctrine of the life of the human person. The theory of this book should be of help in evaluating and intelligently articulating the manifold viewpoints of modern pastoral theology.

Josef Goldbrunner

PART ONE

FOUNDATION

CHAPTER I

The Pastoral Task

LATE IN THE evening a priest sits at his desk—he has just
been appointed pastor of a newly established parish. That day
he went out to explore the territory the bishop had assigned
to him, and tried to grasp the sociological structure of the people over whom he now has a religious responsibility. His new
task as pastor is to absorb himself into this group of Catholics
—of varied religious backgrounds—who have moved into this
area. He must lead them toward faith, mold their Christian
life and form them into a new community, into a parish. As
a curate he learned a great deal about pastoral care from various superiors. He realizes, however, that this new task is much
more complex and demanding: he is now independent in his
planning, approach, means and goals. The task of pastoral
care suddenly looms before him as a new urgency. To serve
as a mere assistant in a parish where another bears the full
responsibility is certainly not the same as being the official
shepherd of the flock. He himself is now challenged in his role
as a human and religious being. The spiritual growth of his
people depends to a great extent on how he will provide the
nourishment they need in their Christian life. There can be
no escape into the mere technicalities of method, for the funda-

3

mental question of pastoral activity itself is at stake. In order to begin a fruitful work within the parish, a pastor must have a clear understanding not only of the "how" of pastoral care, but also of "what" pastoral care actually is.

A glance at the theology texts of his seminary days makes it obvious how much the science of pastoral care has borrowed from other disciplines. One of these is Canon Law, that is, the legal order the Church has given herself in the course of history. Thus this legal aspect in diocesan administration is both concrete and necessary; however, if it were only this, then pastoral theology would be merely an appendix of Canon Law. Juridical principles actually comprise only the minor part of genuine pastoral care, even though this does not always hold true. Pastoral care is all too often carried out merely according to juridical demands—and this remains a temptation today. While it is true that faith depends to some extent on the order of Canon Law, the real essence of faith is not based on juridical concepts and ways of thinking. Pastoral theology, therefore, should be established within the science of theology and should have its own axioms, concepts, principles and categories.

Pastoral theology has borrowed from dogmatic theology, maintaining that the teaching about the Church and the sacraments is actualized by pastoral theology; that pastoral theology *is* applied dogmatic theology; and that the effectiveness of the Church is equivalent to pastoral theology. This viewpoint, too, is often found in practice—most conspicuously, the kind of sermons wherein the hungry faithful are nourished with dogma instead of the bread of the Word. Between a theology thus translated into practice and the actual concrete needs of man, there is a gap that might be likened to a missing floor in a house. The dogmatic way of thinking does not correspond to the nature of pastoral theology, a theology that does not ask for a translation of dogmatic doctrine but rather wants to know its relationship to human nature; for its task is not merely to convey knowledge but to alter human nature so that faith can be established. Therefore, more than ever before, emphasis should be placed on the fact that pastoral theology must start with man himself. Since it is co-ordinated with man's spiritual life, pastoral theology must derive its categories from the relationship between Revelation and the nature of man—of man, however, who is created as being for God.

Pastoral theology has borrowed from the science of liturgy. We can still see this in present-day theological training, where often the professor of liturgy retains his pastoral duties. This results in a combination of the history of liturgy and an individually colored, more or less extensive personal experience in pastoral care. True, the evolution of liturgical forms provides much material for practical pastoral care, but the historical viewpoint alone cannot tell modern man how to find access to liturgical forms. The precise pastoral-theological question, for instance, is not how the form of the Mass has evolved and what the individual prayers mean, but rather how the faithful should be introduced into the mystery celebration and how they can participate in it. But this requires more than a mere knowledge of liturgy. It calls for an awareness of the link between human nature and the mystery celebration; also the link between transparency and the capacity for symbols, which are human prerequisites for the celebration of the liturgy. Thus mystagogy, one of the paramount tasks of pastoral care, once more places the main stress on human nature.

Finally, pastoral theology has also borrowed from moral theology and, even more, has become its handmaid—an indoctrinator of ethical norms, commandments and laws. Yet, out of its own skepticism, a moral psychology[1] (which takes on the task of telling us *how* man can develop and what he can

---

[1] See Theodor Müncker, *Die psychologischen Grundlagen der Katholischen Sittenlehre* (Düsseldorf, 1953).

become) has become affiliated with moral theology (which tells us what *must* be). Here the consideration of human nature enters into theology, admitting that often man must first grow into his obligations and that, if he cannot yet do what he ought to do, he nevertheless should not be morally condemned. Pastoral theology is closely related to this dynamic interpretation of the spiritual life, not only in the ethical realm, as it is here, but also in all spheres of the reality of faith. Therefore moral psychology could build bridges for the understanding of pastoral theology as a discipline in its own right. But ethics is not the same as pastoral care; thus moral theology has to serve pastoral theology.

But just as moral theology gathers around itself all other disciplines of theology—even psychology—as auxiliary sciences, so from the standpoint of pastoral theology not only these sciences, but also moral theology itself, must, like a servant, help clarify theoretically, practically and with proper principles the prime concern of the Son of Man, namely, to impart faith to man. All theological disciplines contribute to this, but none with a view proper to pastoral care.

It is small wonder, then, that the priest at his desk asks himself: "Is there a book in existence that would assist me in my work, a book that would not merely give me general outlines but help me to interpret and order my own experiences and to find a substantial foundation from which I can work?" First of all, such a book would have to be written in the immediacy of experience. This means that it should not be immediately practical with concrete instructions, but that its theories should be taken from, and directed to, areas where pastoral and educational work is being done. The frequently "missing floor" between theology and man should be constructed where the encounter between Revelation and man is experienced, where the contact between God and man takes place. Correlated with this are two sources in accordance with the immediacy of experience.

The first source is modern man's situation in salvation history as taught by biblical theology. This broadens the horizons of salvation history from a view of creation to that of palingenesis, wherein the historical present occupies a very definite place—and this is the decisive point—that is accessible to Christian experience. Man as historical being is the object of pastoral care.

It is in this milieu of salvation history that the pastor addresses men. Their human nature acts and reacts in a universally human way, yet time-bound, that is, related and directed to a specific situation. And the knowledge of this human reality constitutes the second source. Its material is provided by modern anthropology. Both sources of knowledge, the situation of salvation history as well as anthropology, find their mirror image in the self-understanding of man, which concisely can be called consciousness. Its typical, universal and universally understandable elements must give the starting point for the theology of pastoral care and religious education.[2] As long as pastoral care keeps in touch with consciousness, it remains in the immediacy of experience. Consciousness is, it could be said, its regulative element. The pastor must take this consciousness into account; he meets it as an actuality and his problem is how he can influence it with the Christian message.

---

[2] In the following expositions the term "pastoral care" also implies religious education taken in a general sense.

CHAPTER II

Structure-Lines of the World-Concept

IN THE consciousness of man there are patterns, ideas and perceptions that again and again assert themselves and thus form the structure-lines of the world-concept—a kind of blueprint from which man constructs his own world-image. One such structure-line is the duality of spirit and matter,[1] which reaches deeply into the religious area. Even though today natural science is breaking up matter, and existential philosophy ascribes to human spirit merely an existence within the body, this duality is nevertheless experienced in the same way as we still experience the reality of the *four* elements—earth, fire, water and air—in spite of the fact that today science has discovered more than a hundred of them. And thus the experienced duality of spirit and matter molds consciousness. Besides the elements of science, the anthropological elements preserve their validity as *Gestalt*. Everyone, for instance,

---

[1] In his essay, "Sachhafte oder personhafte Struktur der Welt," in *Interpretation der Welt* (Würzburg, 1965), Michael Schmaus opposes false identifications and false separations of spirit and matter.

knows that water is composed of hydrogen and oxygen and yet perceives water as an element, as something elementary, as a unit, a *Gestalt* correlated with human nature. Therefore, such elementary *Gestalt*—images and ideas—found in the consciousness comprise a reality that cannot be explained away by breaking them up into their components. Even the inadequate interpretation of *prescientific* cannot weaken their impetus. Scientific orientations, however, tend to obliterate these universal images found in the depth of the human psyche, thereby causing inner disorientations and the uprooting of natural processes.

Pastoral care, however, is orientated toward the universally human, fundamental structure, and thus the solution does not consist in an either/or: either devaluation and abandonment of the so-called prescientific views for the sake of a purely scientific, mainly abstract (and therefore unimaginable) world-concept, or a similarly one-sided rejection of the scientific development for the sake of a purely human, unchangeable view of nature. The solution consists in an as-well-as: in spite of today's knowledge of nature, the Gestalt-like ideas demand their right-of-existence; even more, both should be led to a harmonious union.[2] Modern man has a particular yearning to be reached in his universally human existence and wants a clarification and interpretation of that which more or less clearly forms his consciousness. Consciousness as a psychic actuality is the field of pastoral care.

One of the most effective prime-ideas is the duality of matter and spirit. With its different manifestations, against, with, and even toward, one another, it runs like a structure-line, or ground plan, through the consciousness of man and forms the world-concept. Two interpretations of the relationship between spirit and matter, the Platonic and the Christian, provide in

[2] See, for example, the dimensions of "above" and "below" in Josef Goldbrunner, "Wege zur religiösen Erfahrung," *Katechetische Blätter* (June, 1965).

their juxtaposition the starting point for a science of pastoral care.

1.

The following diagram might serve as illustration:

·
_____
·

We see here two points, one being clearly above the other. They are separated by a line, without direct connection to each other. Their relationship is fixed, static. When we identify these two points with the structural elements, matter and spirit, as existing in the consciousness, we have a closed world-interpretation.

Above the line we have all that is spiritual: concepts, truths, the human psyche, angels, God. Below the line is matter: material, earth, fire, water, air, bones, flesh, body. Spirit is superior, more valuable; matter is subordinated, inferior. Spirit is good, matter is evil. Spirit is eternal, matter disintegrates, disappears. The soul is immortal, the body perishes. End and aim will be purely spiritual. Spirit and matter, therefore, are in a hostile relationship to each other; they are in principle different and separated, unchangeable and static. They are by nature without any affinity and openness to each other. When, in spite of this, they have to deal with each other, it becomes something that actually should not be and something that points to a catastrophe in the past. Hence, they are constantly at war, like enemies. Spirit is hampered by matter; the soul is enchained by the body. The *dualism* between spirit and matter received its most precise and valid formulation in Plato's idea of the "body as the prison of the soul." When we extend dualism beyond man into a dualism between the world and God, we find the world-concept of the dualistic religions. The question of the why of this contranatural combination of spirit and matter finds its answer in the allusion to primeval catastrophe and punishment.

The corresponding rule of life tends to free the spirit from its defiling mixture with matter by way of *flight from the world*. A necessary transition for this is the separation of the soul from the body so that it can strive toward the sphere of pure spirit, of the pure spirits, the pure ideas, or, in Christian formulation, toward *heaven*. Such a consciousness is characterized by an arrow pointing upward—indicating ascent.

The *schema of ascent* as structure-line of the world-concept corresponds to an experience of the conflict between matter and spirit, which repeatedly imposes itself upon the mind: it happens in the struggle of the human spirit against the natural elements; it happens in man's own human nature, in the conflict between body and soul. The schism between the world and God is also a constant threat. The dualism between spirit and matter, therefore, corresponds to an archetypal experience of man and stamps his consciousness. It will necessarily keep on asserting itself in individuals as well as in collective spiritual tendencies. It existed even before Platonism or Manichaeanism came into being; in fact, Manichaean attitudes are still influential today in the lives of both Christians and non-Christians alike, no matter how enlightened the times and how reason-directed the individual may be. The schema of ascent as a figurative schema of thought is bound to human nature and molds itself, though more or less consciously, in the consciousness at its very depth. Whether this has always been so or how it came into being is of little consequence here: consciousness is the actuality with which the pastor is confronted.

Consequently, education stresses only the education of the spirit. The body is considered only as a container that must function well so that the work of the spirit will not suffer.

Thus the good news of salvation is merely a segment of the whole, namely, that the soul gets to heaven. The world is merely a waiting room for heaven, or an examination hall where moral accomplishment is graded as a requisite for entering heaven. Such pastoral care has a purely tactical relationship to the world.

The schema of ascent as a structure-line affects all levels of spiritual life. This becomes especially evident in the liturgy, for example, rites and ceremonies are no more than necessary wrappings, aesthetically beautiful, with an interesting history; but they can be performed either quickly or slowly, even in an unintelligible language. None of this is essential, of course, if a liturgical rite is only the shell of what is real, the spiritual, or the invisible grace. That alone is the goal of piety! Philosophically the schema of ascent can be formulated as *spiritualism,* which in a strange reversal—as in an overcompensation—time and again causes a wave of materialism, an indication that spirit and matter cannot get rid of each other.

The pastor is confronted with the psychic reality of those entrusted to him, whether faithful or not, as stamped by the schema of ascent. He must reckon with the possibility that his message is understood in the sense, and on the level of, the schema of ascent. That this is actually a widespread and frequent occurrence is as much a fact as is the need of a long and repetitious process in order to transform the figurative schema of thought from its dualistic ascent into a Christian way of thinking. For the human psyche is both, *anima naturaliter* and *christiana et pagana.* The process of a constant transformation is the scaffolding of the conversion process and a never-ending task in the life of the faithful.

2.

Opposed to the pre-Christian schema of ascent is the Christian *schema of descent.* It is not based on natural experience and recognition but on the Revelation of the descending God.

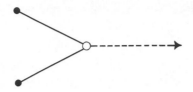

Here again two points indicate spirit and matter, the two structural elements of the world—one above, the other below; but they are on their way, in motion, one toward the other. Their relationship to each other is dynamic. They form a new unity, and the arrow indicates that the movement continues. Just as the points are moving toward each other, spirit and matter are by nature co-ordinated to each other. The material is open for the spiritual; the spiritual is not only capable of moving into matter, but is by nature open to the material. There is no hostility between them, rather an *affinity*.

Spirit-in-matter is not a contradiction in itself, not something that should not be. Rather both are friendly structure-elements, constantly moving toward each other, toward a new one—a third one. The dualism is replaced by a *synthesis,* which in the form of a curious union of the spiritual and the material represents something new. The spiritual comes down into or descends, moves into matter, assimilates it, raises it to a new level, transforms it into expression—and the spiritual becomes visible. Matter becomes the expression of the spiritual, which shines through; matter becomes transparent. An artist's conception of a piece of art, for instance, immerses itself in the marble and becomes visible. Or, a thought confides itself to sounds and becomes audible. "The angels listen with delight to every word of man," says Theodore Häcker, in view of the fact that for the pure spirits the "marriage" of spirit and matter is something new, a wonderful new creature. The figurative representation of this descent of the spiritual is an arrow pointing downward, so that here we can talk of a schema of descent. The rule of life derived from the schema of descent does not advise flight from the world or see as its goal the separation of body and soul in death and a purely spiritual existence in heaven. Death cannot end the relationship to the world but will be the transition to *resurrection*.[3] Thus eschatology becomes the gateway to a full understanding of the doctrine of faith; and reducing eschatology to a mere meaning of heaven is no longer valid. The world is accepted on principle, and thus flight from the world is superseded by a *configuration of the world*. The world is no longer merely a waiting room, but a building site for the new creation.

When we try to formulate the structure-line of Christian interpretation of the world, we are offered the image of the becoming-flesh of the spiritual. Something spiritual, for instance, the soul of a human being, takes on flesh, becomes flesh, becomes incarnated. The structure-line of the Christian world-concept, according to the schema of descent, could be called *incarnation,* just as spiritualism corresponds to the schema of ascent. In the case of Christ Himself—the supreme Spirit, the second Person of God, "God of God, light of light, true God of true God"—it was an immersion of the divine Spirit into matter. According to the doctrine of the hypostatic union this is not only possible, but "everything is created unto" this being-man (Col. 1:16). The structure-line of the schema of descent finds its confirmation through God Himself. "Spirit-in-world"[4] can be placed in the foreground as the basic concep-

---

[3] The dogma of Mary's bodily assumption into heaven points up, in this context, its anthropologic significance. It reminds us of the actual end of man: the resurrection of the flesh.

[4] Cf. Karl Rahner, *Geist in Welt* (München, 1957).

tion of the world as creation. Incarnation is its pivotal point (*caro cardo salutis*).[5]

Consequently, education can be viewed as a help for the incarnation of the psyche; and religious education, as well as pastoral care in general, as a help for the incarnation of the divine reality in man—"Grant that . . . we may be made partakers of His divinity, who has condescended to become partaker of our humanity" (*Ordo missae*).

Pastoral care has to begin by first grasping both the schema of ascent and the schema of descent as clearly separated, and then questioning their relationship to each other. The more or less conscious, yet effective, schema of ascent confronts the schema of descent in the Christian proclamation of faith. The whole scale of reactions, the transition from the unbelieving "no" to the slow, hesitating "yes" of redeeming and liberating faith; relapse and new start; progressive penetration of the schema of descent into new areas of life, together with an ever-developing concept of the Christian world—all these possibilities and tasks compose the pastoral theological theme of spirit and matter, soul and body, God and world, formulated by St. Paul as *sarx* and *pneuma*. To lead consciousness away from the schema of ascent toward the schema of descent is the starting point of pastoral care and Christian education in the immediacy of experience, which means to conform to the structure-line of the Christian world-concept and follow the principle of incarnation.

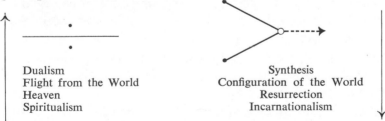

Dualism	Synthesis
Flight from the World	Configuration of the World
Heaven	Resurrection
Spiritualism	Incarnationalism

[5] Cf. Alfons Auer, *Weltoffener Christ* (Düsseldorf, 1963), p. 760; Johannes B. Metz, "Caro Cardo Salutis," *Hochland,* 55 (1962), 97–107.

CHAPTER III

Incarnation as Structure-Line of the Christian World-Concept

WHEN THE IMMERSION of the spiritual into matter is pursued at all levels of existence, it results in a coherent world-concept that, since it is based on Revelation, proves itself fruitful in pastoral care.

Even at the lowest level of existence lifeless matter shows its plasticity. Michelangelo imprinted ideas and proportions on shapeless, heavy marble blocks that soared to form the lofty dome of St. Peter's basilica. In other words, the stone began to speak. The marble dome is an expression of majesty, of unification, of flowering. As spirit speaks through the stone, stone becomes transparent. Stone is capable of expressing ideas; it is ennobled and becomes a work of man. Art is the model for the plasticity of matter through spirit.

Or, an artist takes a violin—a mere product of wood and strings—and draws from it sounds "as from another world." Material is capable of this elevation. Art is on the move to-

16

ward a world wherein the plasticity of matter is played upon to its utmost.[1]

In both cases spirit fuses itself into the material and forms something new, a fascinating work of art; it becomes visible and audible spirit. Although on this level it does not become flesh, but stone and sound, it nevertheless follows analogically the same principle of incarnation and creates a new union. The inclination of the spirit toward the world of matter in all spheres can be paralleled to the structure-line of incarnation. Human spirit, active in creation, transforms the world into a dynamic building site of development: wilderness becomes a cultured land, a world of man, related to man, serving but also calling him to ever new possibilities of spirit and world. Thus the structure-line pervades every work and makes of the world a coherent concept.[2]

On the next level of existence, the vegetative life, or the soul of the plant, the *anima vegetativa,* assimilates matter and transforms it into organic life; the rose, for instance, with its color and fragrance can express what men feel. On the animal level the soul of the animal, the *anima sensitiva,* comprises the entire realm of vegetative life and in addition the capacities specific to the animal. Man sees the lion, the eagle and the horse as planted into matter; yet in their power of expression he recognizes something familiar.

Human spirit, or the psyche of man, the *anima intellectualis*—comprising all dispositions of the *anima vegetativa* and *sensitiva,* yet combined with the specific human dispositions—takes on flesh, transforms the matter into a body, and *I myself* appear. The body is transparent for myself: I speak, I give thanks, I am body, my body.

---

[1] Art, therefore, always contains an eschatological element: it creates an awareness of the plasticity of matter and awakens presentiments of higher possibilities.

[2] Cf. M. Chenu, *Pour une theologie du travail* (Paris, 1955); G. Thils, *Theologie der irdischen Wirklichkeiten* (Salzburg, n.d.).

That the divine Spirit, the second divine Person, desired to come down into matter and assume flesh has already been revealed to us, and this Revelation encourages us to look for the incarnational structure-line in the world-concept. Was it God's humility or was it joy in the new creation, the artwork of spirit-in-matter, that caused the Son of God to become Man? St. Paul seems to share the latter opinion when he says that God is the head of creation, "everything is created unto *him*" (Col. 1:16).

But the most remarkable plasticity of matter in a human body reveals the resurrected Christ in His glorified body.[3] The title "Firstborn of the New Creation" points to the extension of the structure-line of incarnation—even though it can be represented only by a dotted line. Thus the final chapter of Christian anthropology, as well as the final statement about creation, should be derived from eschatology. The universal resurrection of the flesh is connected with the transformation of creation into a new heaven and a new earth,[4] into the "radiant dwelling of God among men." Spirit-in-world is the goal; the fulfillment of the world through the open presence of the Spirit of God is the state of perfection; the full incarnation of God in creation is the Kingdom of God—that which "is prepared from the beginning of the world" (Matt. 25:34).[5]

Incarnation offers itself as a consistent structure-line of a Christian world-concept and permeates all levels of existence (even when incarnation is effected merely in an analogous way). It treats creation, redemption and palingenesis as a whole, as beginning and end, and sets herewith the Christian view in clear contrast to every kind of natural religion, equal to the contrast between the schema of descent and the schema of ascent.

[3] Cf. Hans Eduard Hengstenberg, *Der Leib und die letzten Dinge* (Regensburg, 1955).

[4] Cf. "Lesson 135," *A Catholic Catechism* (New York, 1957).

[5] The Apocalypse, speaking about the "measuring" of the Kingdom of God, of the dimensions of the heavenly city Jerusalem, seems to refer to this when it says "man's measure that is the angel's measure."

Both are figurative schemata, models of thought and perception, able to penetrate all areas of life; they are effective, like hidden switchboards, for all the events of life. The schema of ascent corresponds to the naive, unaffected experience of nature (more exactly of nature in a certain phase of salvation history): it determines the natural religious manifestations. The descent is to be derived from the Revelation of God, according to which Christian consciousness is to be formed.

So should Christian pastoral care follow the structure-line of incarnation. Its task is to encourage the incarnation of the divine life in man so that he may participate in the divine nature.[6] To condition human material to be receptive to divine life, to induce that divine life to assume flesh in human material—this is pastoral care. According to the schema of descent, God will descend and dwell among the men who searchingly and lovingly open themselves to Him.[7] To serve the faith of man means, in this context, to show the way and act as mediator for the incarnation of Christ in man so that he "put on the Lord Jesus Christ" (Rom. 13:14). The entire process of the proclamation of the salvific gifts and their mediation is based on one principle, incarnation. The statement is ventured that incarnation is the principle of every striving for Christianization, the principle of the theology of pastoral care.[8] The theory of pastoral care as well as the bases of pastoral practice can readily be determined by the principle of incarnation.[9]

[6] Offertory of the Mass: "Eius divinitatis esse consortes. . . ."
[7] Cf. John 14:23.
[8] If "incarnation," as the principle of a theory of pastoral care and Christianization, is linked with the dogmatic teaching of the Church, we could come to the ecclesiological formulation that the life of the Church is effected through incarnation.
[9] In this context we refer gratefully to Franz Xavier Arnold, the founder of scientific pastoral theology, who, though in a different formulation, verbalized this principle for the first time, thus giving the science of pastoral care its basis. In his book *Grundsätzliches und Geschichtliches zur Theologie der Seelsorge* (Freiburg, 1949, 1965), he speaks about the "principle of the divine-human," which already contains all elements of incarnation.

CHAPTER IV

The Sphere of Person

1.

THE INCARNATION of the spiritual in material takes place in a different yet analogous way at each level of existence. These differences give evidence to the particulars of an incarnation-orientated pastoral care. The marble block of the sculptor has a passive attitude toward the idea of the artist; yet, in spite of its hardness it is receptive to the spiritual, but this must be imposed on it with hammer and force. The finished work of art constitutes a union of matter and idea, not only externally—as if the forms of the figure would lead to the conclusion that something spiritual has been at work—but, in addition, the very idea has become present. A true mixture has taken place. Nor is the stone merely the garb of an artist's idea, for the idea is not merely present in a concealed way but also has become visible through the stone, visible in the stone. The stone has become transparent for the spiritual. The spiritual is represented through the stone itself, through its participation in it. Thus their union represents a medium between both: a new unity, the work of art. The work of art as a new creation is a constant proof that the duality of the

20

two structural elements of the world, spirit and matter, is capable of a synthesis; it is an indication of the possibility of the schema of descent—spirit takes on stone, stone becomes spiritual.

While lifeless matter, the stone, needs a third party and his skillful strength in order to be united with the spiritual, this process takes place on the next higher level, the world of the plants, by means of the very powers of the vegetative soul. The entelechy of the *anima vegetativa* assimilates the minerals of the soil, transforms and raises them to organic life. However, this happens within a preconditioned cycle of seed, flower, fruit and again seed. Thus the power of incarnation moves within a fixed course, that is, in the realm of the vegetative. It is closed against other areas.

The same can be said of the world of the animal. In addition to all capacities of the lower level, the *anima sensitiva* comprises others specifically proper to it, namely, the power of procreation, of sensory perception, of the capacity to learn and to remember, and even a certain kind of consciousness. But the animal remains imprisoned within itself, in its instinctively patterned course. Yet in the case of the animal there is an opening: in associating with man it is able to grow beyond the purely animal, and in attachment and devotedness it can serve man. Here animal is open to the next higher level of existence, the human.[1] It is open as if the being is on its way to wake up and to reflect. The world of the animal points in this direction, but it cannot go further.

2.

Man, however, is different. He not merely looks around himself, as animals do, but also looks into himself. Thus a

[1] Cf. Thomas Aquinas' statement: "Inferior natura in suo summo attingit ad aliquid infirmum superioris naturae . . ." (*De Veritate,* q.15, a.I). This statement about man applied here to the animal is, of course, to be considered merely analogous.

new dimension opens up. In the hierarchical structure of creation he is the first being who knows that he knows. His consciousness reflects on itself and recognizes itself; it has become
someone who knows about himself—an individual. The consciousness has received a center that rises above the predeter-
mined course of psychic life; it can take itself in hand and do
something with itself. This is a new stage of being, and the
question is posed whether the human psyche with its intellectual, sensitive and vegetative powers is completely absorbed
in the body, as in the case of the plant and animal, or whether
a surplus of the spiritual over matter creates the possibility
that the psyche can at times live without being formed into a
body, by virtue of this new dimension of self-possession. This
self-possession makes possible four essential things.

When the soul takes on flesh in the human body, forming
the body while incarnating itself, it unites with matter in such
way that matter does not merely become its shell. The union
is much more penetrating for it allows the organism to participate in self-possession. The body itself becomes this *someone.*
In shaking hands with another, not only an organic part of
this body is touched, but that one himself. He is his body, not
only its possessor. Yet this body is not only organism but also
the one who lives and participates in the new capability of
self-possession. With this, as *someone,* he is—in spite of external parallels—raised above the level of animal existence and
is not to be understood merely from below (as a purely
organic way of thinking tries to demonstrate).[2] He reacts as
someone, even in sickness,[3] in fortune or misfortune.

Secondly, self-possession enables man to intervene in his
own incarnation. This becomes visible in the body when, for

---

[2] See, for instance, the anthropological writings of Arnold Gehlen.

[3] Medical science uses such recognitions to find a new basis for its
strivings. See Christian Paul, "Zur Phänomenologie des leiblichen
Daseins," in *Jahrbuch für Psychologie, Psychotherapie und medi-
zinische Forschung,* VII, 1/2 (1960), 2–9.

example, we compare the face of a sportsman, expressing exuberant health, with the face of a mother who, pale yet wide awake and glowing with joy, comes from the side of her sick child who has passed his crisis. The material of the face is so plastic that the spirit actually shines through. But how different are the underlying attitudes and experiences! Or let us compare the face of an individual who escapes from every decision he must make with the face of one who disciplines himself, who confronts his decisions with courage, generosity and humility. On the human level, incarnation does not take place simply in a biological way. Because it is not an automatic process many get stuck, and others go astray. The incarnation of the human psyche demands collaboration. It can move toward perfection only by virtue of its own deliberate effort.

Thirdly, while it is true that self-possession creates an independence from the closed cycle of natural events, these external situations cause this *someone* to take a definite stand, to make a decision and to act. A succession of incidents will result from an action taken. This start then is an actual beginning of something new, something that was determined as an effect within a chain of causes. For this *someone* could have made an entirely different decision. Therefore, he has made a creative beginning. It is as if existence, in the self-possession of his human psyche, has reached a level permitting creative activity, which enables him to make beginnings—mysteriously, like God—by his own free decision, even though in a quite different, but analogous way. This means that self-possession of the human psyche activates the power of one's own free decision.

This opens within man a dimension in which this *someone* lives, so to speak, as the center of the psyche (on the throne of the castle of his soul). Making this the basis of his life, man is capable of creative freedom. Beyond the psychic sphere the sphere of *person* opens up. While in the psychic realm man is still able to be psychologically calculated, psychology is no longer competent in the sphere of *person,* since freedom means that no one knows beforehand how that *someone* will decide. In this centralization process of the being, where the core of psychic powers is formed, one moves away from the phase of thingness and reaches the phase of *personal being*. A being with such a core is *person*,[4] just as God is *Person*, in so far as both can make true, free, creative and responsible beginnings. The human psyche is *personal being*, which in its incarnation raises matter to participation in *personal being*.[5] The plasticity of matter allows *personal being* to become flesh.[6] But from this follows also that incarnation on the human level is a *personal* event—it takes place in the *personal* sphere.

3.

Modern man's striving to do something in a personal way expresses his desire to escape the masses, as well as collective thinking, and to find solid footing. Person is felt as an antipole to mass; personal life is seen as the countertendency to collective life, to the universally experienced pull of being leveled to the life of civilization. Man's desire to remain himself and his search for self-realization are the reaction of modern man's awakened power of suggestion in the civilized atmosphere, the condition and intensity of which is determined by the media of public communication.

We can pursue this type of reaction as well in religious sensitivity, where man no longer can or wants to rest in a formal eccelesiastical atmosphere, as he did in the past, but tries to understand himself as an individual and feels that he, as person, can find a foothold in a personal relationship with God. "The category of the individual is decisive for the future

[4] Alois Guggenberger writes about the history of the concept "person" in his essay, "Person," in *Handbuch theologischer Grundbegriffe* (München, 1963), II, 295–305.

[5] See Michael Schmaus, "Sachhafte oder personhafte Struktur der Welt," in *Interpretation der Welt* (Würzburg, 1965), p. 698.

[6] "Matter is not only capable of spirit, related to spirit, but potentially personal" (see Schmaus, *ibid.*).

of Christianity," wrote Sören Kierkegaard in 1859, more than a hundred years ago. To become an individual—that is the phase through which the world and Christianity still must pass! The individual is our great hope; he is the source and fountainhead! For Christian individuality wants to incorporate itself into God-given communities and societies.[7] This means the Christian wants to do it as *person,* in personal actions and attitudes.

These concepts of individual and *personal* necessarily must be defined and cleared from all misinterpretations—particularly as they relate to the common, ambiguous usage of the terms person and personality and of the term "personal" (that is, something that is characteristic of me or certain possessions that belong to me).

In common usage, therefore, one can bring a personal message, but this can as yet be far removed from a *personal* action. *Personal* in an existential sense is more than "personal" in a psychological sense. When we say that one is "personal," psychologically speaking, we mean only that he is interested, that his atmosphere is borne by his feelings, that he has an individual tone in his speech, cultivates his relationships in an individual way. All this takes place on the psychological level, which means that his attentiveness and emotions are present and perhaps colored by his individual character. What happens "personally" in this sense lies merely in the foreground of the *personal* sphere, in the purely psychic realm of dispositions and capacities that can be described and labeled by psychology. Thus a highly gifted personality will give his individual stamp to everything, a so-called personal form, and even his religious behavior can be explained on a purely psychological level. A "personal" type of sermon means that it was not impersonal, not without feeling, but that the preacher filled his

---

[7] See Theoderich Kampmann, "Religionspädagogik und Katechetik heute," in *Katechetische Blätter* (May, 1958), p. 197.

message with warmth and emotion, forming it according to his individuality. A communicant's piety may have been trained into a very intensive feeling for Jesus and yet may lack the attitude of genuine piety that is truly *personal*. The opposite of "personal" in the psychological sense is "impersonal," or cold. But the opposite of *personal* in the existential sense is *natural*. Consequently, every psychic emotion can take place on the *natural,* thing-level, regardless of its individual, so-called personal coloring. This means that something must first happen within man so that the psychic sphere can be lived in a *personal* way. It means that in the psyche, over and above the psychological realm, the *personal* sphere must break open, to which all psychic qualities will then be co-ordinated—that the inhabitant of this sphere must become its ruler. Only then man no longer lives merely "personally" but also *personally,* that is, as the real *person* he is. To search for this inhabitant, for this authority within man, is to ask "Where is the *person?*" It is held that man is created as *person,* and that therefore everything in man is a personal reality and everything he does is the act of person; this is scholastic doctrine. However, that this creature—*person*—has a dynamic structure, that is, that man does not evolve like a plant, the existence of which is determined by place, size, color, and so on; that man as *person* represents a unique reality which must first do something with itself in order to be fully existent—is a recently developed concept of *person,* one that only today has moved into the center of interest. Existential philosophy has revealed that it is this curious self-possession of the *person* that effects the existence of man. In this process a person's being has to be directed into action. This process is formulated as becoming existent, as actualization, self-realization and, in depth psychology, as individuation.[8] Only then can we speak about a *personal* life.

[8] Cf. Josef Goldbrunner, *Personale Seelsorge* (Freiburg, 1955), pp. 36 ff. In this context we may mention Gabriel Marcel, Martin Buber, V. von Gebsattel, Ernst Michel, Romano Guardini and Karl Rahner.

Thus an action is *personal* only when man raises himself from mere being and all its natural endowments of individual psychic dispositions, through self-realization, above a merely natural existence, and takes himself in hand, possesses himself. This happens when he is called forth, awakened and asked to respond; in responding he performs a *personal* act and thus the person is more and more actualized and achieves *personal* attitudes. That this process extends over the entire period of maturing, and even longer, presents great problems to pastoral care.

A child is not capable of living on a fully *personal* level, even though this diminutive person may be very charming in his personality, that is, in his individual acts. Certainly, as a creature, he is already a personal reality, but a static reality, for his *person* must first be actualized. This takes place step by step through association with all who teach him, if they are truly interested in him, and call him forth. Children (and also many adults) thrive on their psychic mechanism, but within these psychic processes the authentic core of the person waits to be addressed, to be called forth, usually in parental love. The child is then drawn into a true dialogue; responding in the same objective way, he will be able to take feeble steps of *personal* action by way of the dialogical intimacy with his educator. But he is yet unable to become master of such *personal* action; besides, it is possible only in relationship to the educator. Hence, Michael Pfliegler calls the ethical behavior of a child "obedience-ethics."[9] The largely dormant core of the *person* is not yet a fully responsible bearer of the child's ethical and religious life. What a mother or teacher conveys to the child can be analogically called "obedience for understanding," which means that it is not sustained, and even less agreed to, by the yet undeveloped core of his *person*. But in order to make faith incarnate the *person* must be actualized, and *personal* life is the prerequisite for the incarnation of man.

[9] See Michael Pfliegler, *The Right Moment* (Notre Dame, 1966) p. 52.

4.

Another dimension of the *personal* sphere makes evident a final point of significance. The human psyche can exercise and train itself; it can acquire customs or, for example, memorize a poem to be recited. A teacher can effect this even through force. But in this case the poem becomes merely an exterior possession. The psyche, however, ought to appropriate the poem interiorly; its thoughts should enter the psyche; even more, they should be absorbed by the psyche, should effect a change and gain power within man so that they can be reproduced, made one's own, actualized, realized. Thus the authentic recitation is like an incarnation of the poem. How is this possible? The inner realm of man is not closed within itself, but open. The thoughts of a poem, which one cannot himself produce, and which a more gifted man has written, can find entrance in the realm of the psyche, where they become incarnated. The same holds true for the actor, musician or philosopher. The idea of a great philosopher can assume form in a statesman. Man is capable of incarnating what is ouside of him. The human psyche thus not only has the power to incarnate itself in the body and develop what lies within itself, but can, in addition, incarnate higher realms that lie outside itself. However, this can never be forced; the person must open himself up.

The secret switchboard that controls incarnation within man is freely-willed inclination; only thus does the *personal* sphere open itself. Man controls his own incarnation; consequently, education and every kind of human guidance must make an appeal to that freely-willed opening of the person, to his self-activity, his collaboration, since education is intended to serve incarnation.

The question in terms of pastoral theology is whether the divine can be incarnated in man. That *God* wants to do this has been revealed.[10] That the divine actuality is *personal,* and

[10] See above, p. 19.

that grace itself, which the pastor is to convey, is *personal* (as the "self-mediation of this God"),[11] is dogma. In view of Christianization this means that the *personal,* divine actuality becomes incarnated in the *personal* sphere of man, or—more simply formulated—that the divine *Person* is co-ordinated to the human *person.* Incarnation of the divine, restricted to the psychic sphere (in the conscious or unconscious, the intellectual and emotional realm) is not possible. It can take place only in the *personal* sphere. Thus, pastoral care must take this direction and the laws of *personal* life must be the laws of pastoral theology.

[11] Cf. Karl Rahner's "Gnade," in *Kleines Theologisches Wörterbuch* (Freiburg, 1962).

CHAPTER V

Realization

WHEN INCARNATION is seen as the principle of pastoral care and as correlated with the *personal* sphere, we must ask, first of all, for a criterion making it possible to convert theory into practice, reflection into action. Is there a landmark for pastoral care, a signpost, to indicate that it is on the right road? Can we find a yardstick for correct pastoral activity? We should be able to derive such a criterion from the specific nature of incarnation in the *personal* sphere.

Catechetics, a branch of pastoral theology, has experienced in the past century a development that can be considered symptomatic, for in its search of the right method to engender faith, it reflects all the possibilities through which pastoral care oscillates and, more or less consciously, aims at the center. In it, too, the criterion of pastoral care can be recognized.

A survey of the development of catechetical methods shows clearly the back-and-forth movement between child and teaching materials, subject and object, whereby the genuine polarity of the span between the two could also be formulated, theoretically, in terms of *personal* criteria.

30

Explanation—Knowledge

Before the catechetical renewal at the turn of the century, the catechist was satisfied to read the questions and answers of the catechism, explain the answers and tell the children to learn them by heart. The material covered was then neatly arranged in their memory like objects in a showcase. The communication of this rote knowledge was considered a service to the cause of faith, which was supported half-consciously, half-unconsciously by the religious atmosphere of the environment. The text-explanatory method had directed itself primarily to the rational powers of the child. Using the language of adults, the message reached the child only through the mediation of the question-answer method of the catechism. Between the child and the liturgy, between the child and Scripture, the method acted as a screen. There was a lopsided emphasis on the teaching material; the object, not the subject, determined the method.

Munich Method—Insight

In the twentieth century, psychology also took hold of educational methods, clarifying the psychological basis of knowing. Explanation mediates factual knowledge, but an object is not necessarily known or grasped in its essence through simple explanation. Learning to understand, especially for children, is therefore dependent upon a sound psychological process. The threefold unity of presentation, explanation and application (connected with the two auxiliary steps of preparation and summarization) was introduced into religious education as the "Munich Method." The ancient method for acquiring knowledge of spiritual things—*propositio, explicatio, applicatio*[1]—was now not only repeated as a theory but, above all, made effective. At this stage in the development

---

[1] See J. A. Jungmann, *Handing on the Faith* (New York, 1959). The Young Christian Workers reassumed the principle "Observe, judge, act."

of the method, the accent rested unequivocally upon the subject, namely, the child who, according to psychological laws, could know objects fully. After all, the aim of catechesis does not consist in merely imparting factual knowledge; this still remains as by-product. It rather undertakes to impart a real grasp, that is, an insight into the content of faith.

The Activity Principle—Involvement with the Material

Emphasis on the activity principle—accent on the matter to be taught—brings the educational pendulum from the subject to the object. It postulates that the child himself should contact and work with the material. Through the materials of instruction, both knowledge and understanding should become self-discovery. Handling the material provides the child with a direct contact of the subject-matter which he refuses to accept second-hand. The application of the activity principle uses many techniques:[2] mere questioning if broadened to a genuine student-teacher dialogue; manual tasks, such as drawing or creating craft objects, are engaged in; problems are solved in group work; catechetical dramatics are employed. Consequently this guiding principle may be enunciated: the teacher should not do or give what the child can do or find by himself. Helping the child too much means damage to the child.

In religious education the activity principle is limited in application when Revelation is the theme of the lesson. Revelation cannot be discovered; it can only be proclaimed, that is, authoritatively proclaimed, and listened to. Apart from consideration of this aspect, religious instruction does call for the use of the activity principle, which contributes the following elements toward a positive future development of catechetical method: the child contacts the subject-matter personally and experiences a call to self-activity; his talents and capabilities are awakened to a greater extent. Thus, within the develop-

[2] Cf. Josef Goldbrunner, "Urbilder—Schlüsselbegriffe—Archetypen," in *Katechetische Blätter* (January, 1964), pp. 1–6.

ment of method, a definite direction toward an immediacy of contact with the object is discernible. Catechesis through the sources of Scripture and liturgy brings the freedom of human talents into play and leads to self-government. Catechesis serves faith not merely by imparting facts and insights but also by providing contact with holy things.

Experience—Assimilation

The formulation of the experience principle grew out of opposition to the idea of education as a purely intellectual acquisition of the content. To experience emotionally does not mean merely to know or to understand; it means, beyond this, to allow one's whole self to be touched by an object in the innermost center of one's being. Catechetical method should not only impart understanding about God, but also be an emotional experience of God. Once again, the accent lies not on the object but on the subject, that is, on the interior event in man. The experience is something happening in the center of man to which the exterior world can at best be a stimulant.[3] The subject develops himself if he makes the object his own, assimilating it by giving himself to the experience with all the doors of the senses and the spirit wide open, allowing the object, as it were, to be drowned in him.[4] The enrichment of the child through religious emotional experiences, through reverence and deep involvement, should serve the faith of the child especially in the presentation and application of the lesson. Nourishment is thus given to faith.

Encounter—Faith

The most widely used textbooks treat the question of catechetical methods up to the experience principle.[5] The next step

[3] See Bollnow, "Begegnung und Bildung," in Guardini-Bollnow, *Begegnung und Bildung* (Würzburg, 1956), p. 32.

[4] *Ibid.,* p. 29.

[5] See Michael Pfliegler, *Religionsunterricht;* Jungmann, *Handing on the Faith.*

in the service of faith leads catechesis to the point where existential philosophy and anthropology meet.

The development of the methodological question demonstrates clearly the constant swing of the pendulum between emphasis on the subject and emphasis on the object. Tendencies toward an immediate contact between the two are noticeable in places and instances where they encounter each other. According to this, the tension between subject and object should not be resolved in favor of either one of the two poles but should be endured in the vis-à-vis, in the pain of confrontation. What does this mean in practice? What happens when the catechist not only wants to offer his students a religious emotional experience but also tries to lead them to an encounter with God?

Two billiard balls can merely collide; two ships can pass each other. But man can chance upon a secret of nature; man can *encounter* another (and this is in fact the model from which the elements of encounter can most clearly be grasped). Man can also *encounter* God. What then is necessary for encounter?[6] Externally we observe the following:

1. Two are in motion. (This means that whoever is already interiorly hardened and unable to move is unfit for encounter.)

2. They approach each other from different directions. (Accidental or providential?)

3. They pass each other so that there is a temporary vis-à-vis. (Do they step aside or confront each other? Freedom of decision.)

4. If contact is made, time must be allowed. (Do catechists always allow for this time, or do they disturb by passing to the next chapter, while both parties desire to be exclusively occupied with each other?)

5. After the encounter, they part. (Encounter fades away. What remains?)

[6] Theoderich Kampmann, *Erziehung und Glaube* (München, 1960), pp. 68 ff.

Inside, however, a great deal more is going on, and it is this interior process that the catechist should serve:

1. The other stands still while confronting me. He remains in himself. I cannot assimilate him in emotional experience; I cannot deal and work with him, as I would with material; but I must respond. He confronts my *self,* not my knowledge or my feelings. I cannot use him to my advantage but must take a stand, hold my own, and open myself up—I am put to the test. If I choose to remain open and not to evade the one I encounter, then completely new levels are touched—not my dispositions, but my very basic *self,* where I am grounded in myself, where I am *person.* This is at stake, with him and with me. This would be the deepest contact!

2. This event changes man, for in a unique awareness he comes to his *self,* experiences himself and takes his own stand, so that now he is here, somehow different from what he was before; now he *himself* is present, *he* exists. This peculiar kind of existence is proper to a human being only when his *person* is actualized. Encounter calls forth this actualization and enkindles the most profound being of man. Thus one could say that the experience still takes place in the psychic sphere— that it is a psychic category. But encounter breaks through the psychic realm, and sends its call through it, thus opening up the *personal* sphere where the one *himself* lives. Man comes forth from his very center and actuates his *person.* The character of encounter, therefore, is to call forth the *person.*

If the other—as it should be in religious instruction—is God, if a true encounter between God and the student is to take place, the human person is confronted, and challenged, by the divine. This then is not only the point of decision, but also the moment when (if man does not turn away, which he is free to do) faith is also engendered. But faith is more than knowledge, recognition or experience: it is a genuine contact with God, a reverend, adoring, thankful, loving and faithful "yes" to Him. Faith is then covenant with Him.

If catechists could but bring this about! Which method would have to be applied? Is it possible to aspire to it? Can the catechist create an encounter the way he can arrange an emotional experience? But encounter takes place in the *personal* sphere and presupposes its freely-willed opening. It is the student's free decision whether or not (during his instruction) he will pass beyond the area of thinking, understanding, dealing with the material and assimilating it, and become a part of the directed, spiritual movement that leads to a true confrontation in the encounter. Hence, encounter can never be forced, planned, calculated or controlled. It can be longed for, hoped for and prayed for.[7] Here method reaches its necessary limitations, thus preventing access to the *personal* sphere unless free decision allows the opening. If this should happen, then faith comes forth—which not only catechesis but also every type of pastoral care should serve.

When we generalize the experiences of catechetics in dealing with serving the faith, this means that although knowledge is part of faith, it does not engender it. The sermon that imparts knowledge fulfills its task only provisionally, even if it is constructed according to psychological viewpoints. Nor does pastoral endeavor that tends to magnify pious experiences make very strong, vivid impressions. This way the spiritual life is experienced only in the emotional realm of the psyche but fails to absorb the entire being of man; it is still unreal, not real enough. To say it positively, all levels must be penetrated if faith is to be realized. On the part of the pastor these levels are: explanation, psychological approach, activity-principle and conveying of experience, thus creating the possibility for encounter; on the part of the faithful: knowledge, understanding, self-involvement with Revelation, assimilation and personal response. Both developments show a common tendency: from the periphery toward the center, from the outside toward

[7] *Ibid.*, pp. 85 ff.

the inside, from the part toward the whole; thus the reality of faith embraces the entire man including his *personal* sphere— and here faith is realized.[8] Not only are religious knowledge and pious experience the goal of active pastoral care, but also the realization of faith. To realize comprises conceptually the entire context of catechetical development in its tendency. To help realize faith in others is actually the service of pastoral care. Realization is both way and goal at the same time—goal in so far as the content of faith is not only to be known, thought, felt and experienced, but also incarnated through its union with the Christian. The Christian represents an incarnation of the Word of God.[9] Holy Scripture says "to put on the Lord Jesus Christ" (Rom. 13:14). The way of realization sets two tasks:

1. To make man familiar with the content of faith by the forms of mere instruction up to the point of possibility for encounter. The conditions for this are afforded by the content and mode of proclamation and also by the messenger himself. To work this out is essentially the theory of pastoral care.

2. The listener should become open. This process, too, can run the entire gamut from mere listening to the encounter and free decision. What is necessary for this opening of the person, what help can be given, is part of the thematic theory of pas-

---

[8] The concept of realization is akin to J. H. Newman's term "realize," a central concept of his theory of faith, and can be interpreted as the great switchboard where an idea or a thought is transformed into a spiritual reality within man. The content of the intellectual recognition is worked out and penetrated and its ethical significance responsibly accepted, so that it actually lives in us and generates life. The interior realization urges to exterior action, and with this, recognition finally becomes an existentially personal realization. Werner Becker, in his essay, "Realisierung und Realising," *Cardinal Newman-Studien* (Nürnberg, 1962), V, 269–282, presents both the development and functioning of this concept according to Newman (pp. 270, 271). Newman considers the theological and philosophical aspects of the "realization of faith," whereas the psychological ones are of interest to us.

[9] Cf. Becker, "Realisierung und Realising," p. 271.

toral care. The material needed for this can be drawn from a combination of theology and anthropology. As the measure for the goal and the condition of the way in both theory and practice, realization is the criterion of pastoral care.

The triunity of principle, level of being and criterion—incarnation, *personal* sphere and realization—seems to be the foundation of pastoral theology that gives this theological discipline its own nature, and that prepares the road for a theoretical penetration into pastoral care and religious education. Christianization is incarnation in the *personal* sphere through realization.

CHAPTER VI

Realization in the Light of Salvation History

To REALIZE faith is a task given to Christians in a certain phase of salvation history, the so-called between-time,[1] which is marked by two specific events: Christ's Resurrection and His return. The characteristics of the time between these two events form the present religious situation and, as realities, influence the process of realization. They are actualities that pastoral care must take into account. A view of salvation history reveals four basic points:

    (1) Dimension of future
    (2) Hidden presence
    (3) Burden of the past
    (4) Pain

All four are characteristics or elements of the between-time and create a concrete situation for the realization of faith.

(1) Dimension of future

The situation of the people of Israel in the desert is a model

[1] The "tempus medium" of St. Augustine.

of the architecture of the between-time. How was their faith-consciousness structured? As tribes were on the move, from the captivity in Egypt into the promised land, their situation spanned from the past to the future, between Egypt and the promised land. This was a reality for them, and their faith-consciousness was in accordance with it. One might ask which was more accentuated, the past or the future. Undoubtedly the past was concretely felt in the homelessness of a wandering people, yet the magnet pulling at their consciousness was the promised land. This future provided the strength to endure everything. The past explained the negative aspect of the present, but from the future streamed vital strength. The consciousness of the people was stamped by the future; their religion was a religion of the future. Theirs was a striving for a new state of life—it was dynamic!

This is the model then from which we can learn the way pastoral care should take in forming the faith-consciousness of the Christian. For Christianity, too, is on the move: from a captivity by many fetters (the unharnessed forces of nature, sickness, misery, death and the history of national catastrophes) to another promised land, which Holy Scripture calls the "Kingdom of God." The situation of the liberation from captivity repeats itself in a general way in the life of Christianity and of the Christian. What should also be repeated is the architecture of faith-consciousness, but here, we must admit, the accent is placed more on the past than on the future. The doctrines concerning the cause of our captivity, namely, original sin, our inherited guilt, the act of liberation on the cross—all events of the past—feature more prominently in pastoral care than do the teachings about the future, the proclamation of the coming Kingdom. This influences the realization of faith: we assimilate things of the past differently from those of the future, because the biological and psychical stream of life flows unflaggingly into the future. If this natural dynamic of life were unified with the proclamation of the future dimension by discovering its own relationship to the future, then surely bios, psyche and kerygma would become more and more united, and kerygma then realized.[2]

But a relationship with the dimension of future presupposes the awareness of a fascinating future, as reported in the Old Testament by the messengers Moses sent out: "We went into the land to which you sent us. It does indeed flow with milk and honey, and here is its fruit" (Num. 13:27). And the man who found the treasure in the field was likewise fascinated by what his future would hold if he could buy the field with the treasure in it (Matt. 13:44). In order to realize the dimension of future in the between-time, we must first get a glimpse of this treasure.

In the proclamation of faith, however, such a glimpse is generally presented only in the usual restricted way, that is, as an entering into the ecstasy of union with God, the *fruitio Dei,* the idea of God and the soul and nothing else. Yet this teaching of the ecstatic concept of the final future corresponds to the schema of ascent, and we can easily see why it touches only a part of human nature and why it can be realized only very fragmentarily. Such proclamation of faith excludes the world; the community of men no longer plays a role, for the personal relationship to God in its exclusiveness eschews every third. But is this God's plan of salvation?

He who "brought the message" (John 1:18), the Son of God, gives us a different conception of the future: not the ecstatic, but the incarnational, which includes both the community of men and that of the cosmos.[3] It is God's own will to break through the exclusiveness of the personal relationship

---

[2] Cf. Josef Goldbrunner, ed., *The Dimension of Future in our Faith* (Notre Dame, 1966).

[3] Cf. Alfons Auer, *Weltoffener Christ* (Düsseldorf, 1963), p. 160; Gustav Thiels, *Theologie der irdischen Wirklichkeiten* (Salzburg, n.d.); Rudolf Schnackenburg, *Gottes Herrschaft und Reich* (Freiburg, 1959).

between Himself and man. From this it follows that the way to the Creator leads through His creation, from the gift to the giver, as was seen previously in the proclamation through the description of the new promised land, the Kingdom of God! It follows moreover that man's dialogue with God includes creation in its content; and that consequently the realization of faith is likewise obviously effected in the context of creation.

We shall prove later on that the *personal* sphere is actuated by embracing all realms of creation. Thus religious instruction that aims exclusively, or too directly, at the *personal* relationship between God and man, Christ and Christian, seems to omit intermediate links and make excessive demands on man. The following short description of the Kingdom of God (the coming eon) has five aspects, each with the tendency to point to the giver of such gifts. Indirectly they are concerned with human nature.

1. The Kingdom of God is God's rulership of the *land* that extends over the entire creation. The cosmos is the Kingdom in which God openly gives us the benefit of His dominion, or better, of His ruling power. The effects become evident in creation, in individual man and in communal life.

2. The miracles of Jesus are not only a proof of His divine power, an indication of His divinity (here homilies and catechetics are often found wanting), but in the context of salvation history they also reveal the situation in the Kingdom of God. His calming of the sea, for instance, throws a sudden flash of light on the chains of captivity that man must endure, even though he conditions himself accordingly, namely, the fact that the elements of nature are superior to man and can even kill him. Jesus has the power to free man from this chain. What the Apostles experienced, the superiority of Jesus over the elements of nature, is a sign of the right order between man and nature, the way it will be established in the restored world (palingenesis, Matt. 17:11); in the Kingdom of God it will be as experienced in the miracle.

The miracles of the water changed into wine and of the multiplication of loaves indicate that in His Kingdom there will no longer be misery. The healing of the sick means that where this Savior is master, there is no longer illness. The three miracles that brought the dead to life (the daughter of Jairus; the young man of Naim; and Lazarus, who was already buried several days) prove Christ to be master over death. In His Kingdom there will no longer be death. In retrieving the possessed He shows how He crushes diabolical, contradivine forces, which in His Kingdom will be powerless. The forgiveness of sins manifests His ability to extricate man from his fallen nature, from his enslavement to the cycle of sin and evil.

All these salvific acts of Jesus illustrate the future life in His Kingdom—the promised land—toward which mankind is moving. This Kingdom reflects the captivity with all its chains, from which Jesus leads God's new people. It is the life in the new promised land that retrospectively enables us to grasp the situation of our world, of the second eon, as a captivity. The natural standards to which we are so accustomed acquire a relative meaning when confronted by the concrete indications of the future world that lies above what we call "nature," and thus termed "supernatural." Often the longing for salvation can be awakened only by opening one's imagination to the possibilities of the world in the promised palingenesis.

3. The concrete reality of this new world is manifested by Jesus Himself—the Firstborn of the new world, the resurrected Lord. The Church's liturgical living with the risen Lord during the forty days after Easter is a practice aiming at salvation. The risen Lord is the first aspect of open reality in the new eon, and at the same time the perfect interrelation of matter and spirit, for in Him the plasticity of matter as well as the forming power of the spirit are fully actualized—this is the model of man's future.

4. The promises contained in the seven letters of the

Apocalypse (second and third chapters) are a concise analysis of the self-development of every man:[4]

2:7 —"Him who overcomes I will permit to eat of the tree of life."

He who perseveres in his faith, who faithfully endures his struggles in life, will live forever. Life extends itself consciously into eternity.

2:11—"He who overcomes shall not be hurt by the second death."

He who trusts that he will not be condemned, or abandoned, or excluded from the Kingdom of God, need not fear, for his anxiety can be overcome and the unfolding of life will not be hampered by metaphysical fear.

2:17—"To him who overcomes . . . I will give him a white pebble, and upon the pebble a new name written, which no one knows except him who receives it."

He who can give the individual his authentic name knows his being, confirms it, and calls it forth, so that it experiences the joy of its unfolding. Many never experience this joy on earth. He who bestows the new name, the Lord Himself, knows the being of every individual in his very fullness, calls it forth and con-

---

[4] As an example, we might refer to Romano Guardini, "Der Name des Menschen, Gedanken über die Apokalypse 2:17," in *Kaufet die Zeit aus,* Hermann Kirchhoff, ed. (Paderborn, 1959). Guardini interprets the promise of the new name as "fulfillment of our personal existence," that everyone is completely himself, irrevocably unique and free (p. 20). This interpretation is not so much concerned with the traditional and seemingly established meanings but goes beneath them to the original process of the formation of symbols, which later on have found many, though not always faithful, expressions. The true meaning of the act of naming is the concern of such an interpretation, and not that given by some particular writer. Likewise, symbols, such as the morning star, the shining garment, the column of the temple, the sitting-on-the-throne, should be investigated as to their origin. Then these symbols begin to speak a new language.

firms it in a way that has never been experienced
among men. In relevant terms, one could say that this
name-giving is the guarantee of self-realization and
perfection.

2:28—"I will give him the morning star."

That the experience of the morning star in the freshness
of the morning (youth) finds its symbolic expression in
the heavenly Christ (Apoc. 22:16) is conclusive in
that he who overcomes will have full power of life.

3:5 —"He who overcomes shall be arrayed thus in white
garments."

Something more profound than the ordinary interpretation
of clothing (Eccles. 9:8, Matt. 17:2, Acts 1:10; also garment
of baptism, garment of grace, garment of the angels and saints)
should come to mind when we ask "What is a garment?"[5] A
garment is not only protection but also expression. It should,
in its chosen form and color, befit and express the nature of
the individual. That which is not always possible here on
earth, which must even be concealed and camouflaged,
namely, to reveal one's nature with openness, is in God's
Kingdom promised as reward to him who overcomes: the
revealing of oneself in openness, in self-expression without
any risk.

3:12—"He who overcomes, I will make him a pillar in the
temple of my God."

The irreplaceability of each single pillar in a Greek
temple is a symbol of the irreplaceability, the significance and unique importance of every individual—the
lack of which, in our present life, constitutes intense
suffering for many.

3:21—"He who overcomes, I will permit him to sit with me
upon my throne."

[5] See Erik Peterson, "Theologie des Kleides," in *Marginalien zur
Theologie* (München, 1956), pp. 41–55.

The question asking what makes a man worthy to sit on a throne is answered as follows: The absence of all tension, frustration, awkwardness and narrow-mindedness, as well as the flowering of everything that is free, broad-minded and noble. To be allowed to sit with Him upon His throne is, in addition to all traditional meanings, a promise of the unfolding of man's noble nature.

If the promises in the seven letters are interpreted according to their original symbols, we arrive at a description of individual life that is fascinating for modern man: not only because of its psychological momentum but because of its deeper insight into man, that is, from the anthropological viewpoint.

5. The visions recorded in Chapters 21 and 22 of the Apocalypse offer a fragmentary description of community life in the Kingdom of God.

The Kingdom of God, represented as a city ("the holy city, Jerusalem") not only retains the meaning of the old Jerusalem but also conveys the idea of the well-ordered flourishing community life of a city. Its public life ("the street of the city" [Apoc. 21:21]), contrary to our contaminated, deceptive, impenetrable and often inferior public life, is "pure gold, as it were transparent glass" (21:21).

"And they shall bring the glory and the honor of nations into it" (21:26). All nations will continue with their characteristics and diversities, but their impurity, sickness and sinfulness will be cured by "the leaves (of the tree of life) for the healing of the nations" (22:2). Mankind as a whole will enjoy the divine plan of creation as a variety of nations, as a reflection of the tremendous wealth of God.

Such descriptions of the Kingdom of God, though at first appearing skeptical and bewildering, produce an attraction similar in effect to that which the "promised land" had on the people in the desert. Faith-consciousness is restructured, and the advent-attitude releases its flow toward the future—moreover, a future grasped as a real, true world of man, both in individual fulfillment and in community life.

This dimension of future—as an element of our salvation-situation—can be all the more realized since, in its dynamics, it parallels the biological process of aging and the psychic process of maturing. We shall see that the conscious acceptance of age levels is connected with the future dimension of the salvation-situation and, through a kind of reciprocal effect, that it facilitates the aging process—all in proportion to the realization of this dimension of future. Thus pastoral care provides help for the manifold crises of aging and prepares the way for the message of the Kingdom of God.

The psychic process of self-realization, too, from immaturity to maturity, is constantly moving in openness toward the future. A man without future in his inner development no longer cares,[6] not even for the Kingdom of God. On the other hand, the message of the Kingdom of God offers a future and can awaken the desire for further self-realization. Hence, pastoral care, while stimulating man's desire for self-realization, serves, consequently, the realization of the dimension of future. Service to the Word and service to man are inseparable. Pastoral care is a union of both: the sowing and the tilling of the field; the proclamation of faith and the care of man. Instinctively the faithful look for both from the pastor: the Revealed Word and his counsel in their self-realization; or, in other words, the knowledge of both realities, the divine and the human. It is in relation to the dimension of future, the weakest point in contemporary proclamation, where we see most distinctly the connection that theology and anthropology has in pastoral care.

(2) The hidden presence

The effectiveness of the dimension of future in faith-consciousness finds a frontier in its retroactive effect on the

[6] Cf. Werner Bergengrün, *Der Grosstyrann und das Gericht* (n.d.).

present. Whoever lives only for the future overlooks the present and its tasks; the present for him is not only relative but also depreciated, and becomes merely a life in the desert. But on this point Christendom progressed beyond the Old Testamental model of liberation from captivity, since the Kingdom of God, which Christ has promised, is more than a great event of the future that "will come in its full glory at the Last Day."[7] The Kingdom of God is, at the same time, a great event of the present. It has already begun, is already a reality and here present, and this through Jesus Christ; "but his glory is still concealed."[8] This concealed presence is the second element that should run through faith-consciousness like a structure-line. It is a task of pastoral care.

Ordinarily the hidden presence of the Kingdom of God is played off against its future dimension. The fear of falling into an eschatologism prevents a distinct orientation of the entire message of Jesus toward the future. The result is a weakness in the realization of faith, in that the reality of the doctrine of the Kingdom of God is removed from the elements of time (dimension of future) and of space (transformation of the world in the new eon). What remains is purely religious talk about the Kingdom of God, which in spite of the resonance it evokes in religious sentiments cannot be realized, since it follows the structure-line of incarnation only in part. From the viewpoint of salvation history, the message of the Kingdom of God is conjoined with space and time. The first emphasis on the future event in space and time is, in clear distinction, followed by the second emphasis on the *hidden presence*. Once the future has been discussed, we can understand the present. The

[7] See *A Catholic Catechism* (New York, 1957).

[8] *Ibid.* Here that which becomes effective for the consciousness of faith exegesis calls the "future" and the "present," or "realizing" eschatology. See also *Lexikon für Theologie und Kirche,* III, 1088 (Rudolf Schnackenburg); and cf. P. Hoffmann, "Reiche Gottes," in *Handbuch theologischer Grundbegriffe* (München, 1963), II, 414–428.

flower explains the bud. This also is the natural way to stimulate and realize the relationship to present values. Faith-consciousness thus assumes clear architectural lines that correspond to Revelation as well as to the reality of life and the world: from the present to the future; and from the future back again to an understanding of the present.

The hidden presence of the future can most clearly be discerned in the Eucharist. The bread of the Eucharist is transformed into the reality of Jesus, the risen, the first real aspect of the future Kingdom. The bread is this very life of Christ with all its vital powers: *Panem de coelo praestitisti eis— omne delectamentum in se habentem!* "You have given them bread from heaven—having all sweetness within it!"

Yet this glory is still concealed, covered, hidden under the veil of the mystery-celebration. As in the Eucharist, the vital powers of the coming eon are present, though concealed, in every mystery-celebration of the sacraments. In liturgy our eon has already been renewed; we are being nourished with the powers of the new eon.

To incarnate the hidden reality of the third eon is part of the Christian life. To assist in this incarnation means that pastoral care must reveal what is hidden and make visible what is invisible. The means to this are the word and the actions of the mystery-celebration. Both should become transparent. Man's capacity for symbols should be the bridge between the two. The material of our world allows a glimpse into the new world so that it shines through; word and actions become transparent and reveal the hidden presence of the future. To the degree that proclamation and the signs of the mystery-celebration become clear, they begin to speak and to appeal to man's capacity for symbols: he experiences in a special manner the invisible through the visible.

A symbol, even a symbolic action (for instance, a festive meal) conceals; but in its form and expression it points to the meaning of the concealed. But a symbol is at the same time transparent. The invisible meaning becomes visible, audible, even tangible. It becomes a light within the symbol, as if it were present, and thus illuminates the symbol itself. In a true symbol the invisible can be experienced as reality— but only by one who has the capacity for symbols.

Man as an incarnated spiritual being is capable of symbols: he oscillates between spirit and matter and finds the center in the uniting process of incarnation, so that he himself is the manifestation of something invisible. This results in a kind of ability to be resonant to everything similar, an ability to grasp in the visible that which is invisibly embodied in it.

To be able to see symbols and to experience through symbols—in short to have the capacity for symbols—is the organ for the realization of the hidden presence of the third eon. As an organ, this capacity is subject to the laws of awakening, growth and care, as well as to those of atrophy and damage. On the other hand, modern collective man's defective capacity for symbols should not varnish over the fact that the use of symbols is a primitive and general tendency of the human psyche. In his deficiency he is not content with the external object and in his own mind is prone to questioning the hidden meaning. The search for this meaning, as a psychic function, is put to full service and is led to its goal through the hidden presence of divine powers in the symbols of the liturgy. Liturgical education, therefore, through its inherent orientation to the future, assists human striving in the same way as does the dimension of future. Its concern is a task of pastoral care and its place in a theory of pastoral care will have to be found. The capacity for symbols is necessary for the realization of the second element of the salvation-situation, the hidden presence of the Kingdom of God.

(3) The burden of the past

The proclamation of the Christian message of the Kingdom of God clashes not only with unbelief, but also with difficulties in its realization in the life of the faithful. Time and again man reacts negatively to the Word of God in a number of ways: rejection in disbelief, indifference, aversion to Holy Scripture, recurrent withdrawal from the spirit of the Gospel. Why is it so hard to hold on to the dimension of future? Why does the reality of the hidden presence so easily fade away? Theology explains these shadows as an inheritance of the past, as the consequence of man's fall, which manifests itself in the opposition of *sarx* against *pneuma*—in the *other* law that rules in the members (St. Paul) and in the resistance of the darkness to the light (St. John). These metaphors are concretized in man's ethical failure and, even more clearly, in his reaction to Revelation. Through Jesus man becomes familiar with God's way of life. Man reacts positively and negatively, the latter even more frequently than the former. Why? Does the divine way of life make demands which, while being essential, still require effort of human nature?

The parable of the workers in the vineyard (Matt. 20:1–16) shows us clearly the weak point within man in regard to the divine way. The claim of the workers is based on the idea of wages equivalent to the amount of work done. This gives a sense of security; it can be calculated and read off as from a scale. The relationship between employer and employee has a material character. Whoever confronts the Father of Jesus Christ with such an attitude will hear the words: "I do thee no injustice. . . . Take what is thine and *go*" (Matt. 20:13, 14). He does not understand God. This reaction, however, should be the occasion of a deeper insight. What occurs here is more than justice; here the scale does not rule, but the heart. This, of course, cannot be calculated and allows no room for claims. This magnanimous offer is better expressed with terms like gift, generosity, love. But this means that in the foreground is the giver, and any reference to a wage scale bound by contract becomes insignificant. No claim is made on the donor, but he can be trusted; a favor can be asked of him. It does not, however, give the security of a legal claim; it is rather a risk, a venture. Such should be the attitude when man confronts God. The relationship is raised to a personal level. It becomes Christian when it leaves behind the categories of thingness, that is, that which can be measured, added and subtracted, but rather is concerned with personal values: confidence, supplication, thanks, praise, forgiveness and the like. In this area Christ raises the relationship between man and God from a material to a personal level, and on this level the Gospel addresses man. It has the nature of a personal call. In the realm of the Gospel no material guarantee is required of God, but a personal relationship is engendered, based on the decision of trust, love and faith. Such a personal relationship, also in human affairs, creates a special awareness, an intensity of experience that affects all areas of life. It stirs the feeling that only now is man coming to himself, even though it be transitory periods of elevation followed by the mere recognition that his perfection depends on the continuity of this awareness, this intensity, this coming-to-himself. A relationship with the divine *Person* should call forth the very depths of the human *person* and lead him to complete actualization. The proclamation of the Gospel invites him to take this road of *personal* life; it calls forth the *person* so that he may actuate himself and become able to establish a *personal* relationship with God in a religious attitude that is fully Christian.

Yet, to our surprise, we experience that this effort to be *person* meets resistance, that the call to *personal* life arouses antipathy, even hostility within ourselves. Man is created for *personal* life and the Gospel invites him to it, but he is wearing shoes of lead—a burden from the past. It seems, in terms of anthropology, that weakness in being *person* is the innermost core of our inherited guilt.[9] This weakness, however, is

[9] Cf. Karl Rahner, "Zum theologischen Begriff der Konkupiszenz," in *Schriften zur Theologie* (Einsiedeln, 1962), I, 377–413; Bernhard Stöckle, *Die Lehre von der erbsündlichen Konkupiszenz in ihrer Bedeutung für das Christliche Leibethos* (Ettal, 1954), pp. 147 ff.

an element of our salvation-situation. Our struggle for *per-sonal* life not only contends with strong feelings of aversion, but also finds great difficulty in sustaining the *personal* level, since every *personal* relationship deteriorates from time to time and sinks to the pre*personal* level[10]—symptoms of man's inherited guilt found in all areas of life, but most obviously in his religious life in so far as the Gospel is concerned.

The effort it takes to strive for the *personal* life indicates the degree of weakness in being *person:* the difficulty in raising oneself from the thing-level to the *personal,* the recurring re-lapses, the experience of being seldom or only temporarily capable of *personal* actions, and the experience of not being able to rise at all from the pre*personal* state. Many live in a state of intense actualization of the *personal* sphere, especially on the cultural level, but nevertheless remain deaf to the last call, the call of the *personal* God. Since the incarnation of Christian faith takes place in the *personal* sphere, pastoral care must endeavor to recognize the dangers to *personal* life, must discover the tendencies that hamper and prevent it. Teaching the laws of *personal* life could, therefore, provide insights into *person*-deficiency and into the structural facets of the actualized *person.* The field of work in pastoral care is the life of the *person,* and a doctrine of the *life of person* is simul-taneously the ordering principle and the disposition for a doctrine of pastoral care.

(4) Pain

The salvation-situation of the between-time contains an-other element, which can be found at the point where the new eon touches the present. In the celebration of the Eucharist, where their point of contact is most evident, the cross points out that the mutual interchange of both eons is linked with two experiences, joy and pain—the latter until death. The

---

[10] Martin Buber says: ". . . but this is the noble sadness of our fate that every thou in our world must become an it."

cross is, therefore, the symbol of both victory and death. Even though the pastor's great task is to put the spotlight on spiritual joy (as a matter of fact, joy is encountered surprisingly often among the faithful by one who is alert and has experienced joy himself), this will be less worrisome to him than the element of pain.[11] The more impressive facet of the cross is the dark side: pain in all its variations. And while the pastor should know joy, he must know pain as well, for pain is an element of our salvation-situation. More exactly, it is the element most impressive and palpable to man and, consequently, seems to be predominant in pastoral care.

The meaning of the cross can be learned from the life of Jesus. It is a symbol of the crossing-over from here to there, from this world to the other, from the world of man to the being of God, from this eon to the new eon, from the fallen world to the Kingdom of God. The threshold is death or, more appropriately, the zone of death, which envelops our world like a mantle of air. Jesus, passing through this zone in His death, broke it open, made it crossable, so that, since His death, he who dies is no longer blocked in this zone of death, is no longer held back in the world of the dead, but can cross over. Yet, death remained a threshold, crossable, but nevertheless still there, inescapable whenever our salvation-situation encounters the new eon. This encounter is the event of death itself, and also its effect, that is, the pains that are like metastases of death or the atmospheric conditions of the crossing-over.[12]

[11] It is not up to the science of pastoral care to enter into speculations about pain, its why and wherefore, but rather to consider the experienced fact of pain, which the priest finds in the consciousness of those entrusted to him. Cf. Leonhard Weber, "Theologie und Teleologie des Schmerzes," in *Arzt und Christ*, No. 4 (1958), 204–212; and C. S. Lewis, *The Problem of Pain* (New York, 1943).

[12] The ecstasy of pain in pagan religions is very likely a presentiment of this. Pain, deliberately inflicted to the point that it can be consciously endured, seems to make it possible for one to break through the limits

Christianity, therefore, is able to see all pain in the symbol of the cross or of a "crossing-over." Just as a magnet attracts iron particles, sorting them according to the lines of force, so in Christian life the cross orientates all pain toward the crossing-over. To accept this means to reorientate the concept of pain in one's own consciousness and to let it be caught up in the momentum of the imitation of the cross of Jesus, thus making it fruitful for the crossing-over. To make pain consciously and faithfully a part of our salvation-situation has a modifying effect, which, while it does not lessen pain or make it more tolerable, renders it effective for the reality of faith. This is observable in many kinds of pain.

The change from one critical age period to another causes mental and physical suffering, and the pains of maturing are an aid to the realization of the dimension of future. At the same time, these pains indicate that the maturing presses toward the crossing-over of the threshold.

The pain suffered in acquiring the capacity for symbols, whether it be blindness, a groping inability to grasp or a sudden flash of insight, helps to realize the hidden presence of the new eon in the liturgical rites and also in all other areas of Christian life.

The pains of *personal* actualization focus on the burden of the past and bring it to a head. The *personal* sphere now opens. Here realization can take place.[13]

---

of consciousness and step out of the conscious, thereby making room for "that which transcends the conscious"—the unconscious. It must be taken into account that this intensification of the psyche effected through the deliberate prolonging of the ecstasy of pain actually touches the zone of death with its twofold experience of "death and love." Cf. Charles Morgan's *The Fountain* (New York, 1932), where he expresses the opinion that in pain the significance of life is experienced. The Christian concept of pain is different from the above to the same degree that penetrating the zone of death differs from merely touching it.

[13] Cf. Josef Goldbrunner's "Heiligkeit und Gesundheit," in *Sprechzimmer und Beichtstuhl* (Freiburg, 1965).

Finally, all the extraordinary suffering due to external causes—work, illness, understanding our fellow man and conflicts for the sake of faith—are absorbed by this dynamic power.[14]

The pastor should know, and take into account, that any kind of pain produces a psychological effect, and that in most cases it can be viewed as a phenomenon of the maturing process of *person*. But the point in question here is not psychological, but rather ontological. We are on a different wavelength: the pneumatic sphere. Here we recognize the fact that the event of pain has a course, like the biological aging-process, that continuously influences man, whether he likes it or not, and that its movement can be rendered fruitful through a conscious acceptance and formation. The movement of pain is orientated toward the crossing-over. When the pastor visits a sick person, the movement toward the threshold is actualized, even though the sick person may be unaware of it. But the more the sufferer takes this movement consciously into his life, takes it as his *cross,* or as the imitation of Christ—or in the great context of salvation history comprehends the cross as the symbol of the threshold—the more he opens himself up to what is beyond the threshold, to the powers of the third eon, grace, and the life of grace. Realization is effected to the degree that consciousness yields to this movement of pain and accepts it.

Pain is an inevitable element of the salvation-situation, and of all elements mentioned before (dimension of future, hidden presence, burden of the past) it is the one to which man is most sensitive. Pain attacks man's weakest point, his body. This leads to two consequences.

[14] It is questionable whether this is valid as well for so-called illegitimate pain that stems from one's own false attitude, for instance, from unhealthy asceticism, or pain that is a symptom of neuroses. See also Josef Goldbrunner, *ibid*. The priest should unmask such illegitimate pain and not let it be religiously misused. Since it originates in untruth, it cannot serve the truth or be an element of the salvation-situation.

The first consequence is the impulsive reaction to pain, which can be a kind of stupor for some, a courageous enduring for others, or even a ranting and raving by still others against this "invention." The corresponding spiritual attitudes are resignation to the inevitability of pain, self-controlled suffering in dignity, or that of blaming the Creator for the cruelty and senselessness of this scourge. In contrast to all this, pastoral care points to the cross as a model of suffering as well as the way to the other con. But here again the scope of decisions meets the extremes of a kind of indifferent inability to comprehend and a mocking opposition to love of the cross, and herein lies the lifelong struggle, as well as the effort newly demanded by every pain to suffer faithfully the movement toward the threshold.

The second consequence is that this element of the salvation-situation is prone to degrade faith to the level of the realistic, to the painful, mundane level, and forces the other elements—the dimension of future, the hidden presence, the burden of the past—to adjust to the reality of this world, thus preventing faith from becoming unrealistic. Hence, viewed in the symbol of the cross, pain, as an element of the salvation-situation, furthers the realization of faith.

PART TWO

STRUCTURE

CHAPTER VII

Individuality and Its
Right-of-Existence

1.

Between incarnation—the principle of pastoral theology—and realization—its criterion—the person acts as transformation-center. In the person's life the sphere is opening up, in which Christian faith can be realized. No matter whether pastoral care is based on the content of faith, that is, on *what* is to be incarnated, or on the question as to *how* this can be effected and realized, the control board, in both cases, is the *personal* element, the life of the person, or, figuratively, the *personal* sphere. It is the invaluable foyer for what comes from above. The degree of the pastor's effectiveness is limited to the period of man's growth from infancy to maturity, in which period the possibilities of incarnation of faith and of pastoral care stand or fall, even though there are no limits to the exceptional effects of grace. Thus the core of the following reflections is the actualization-process of the person. Its structure and disposition are based on its component elements.

Man must stand the test and perform his tasks in four areas

61

of life: (1) individuality; (2) sexual love; (3) community; and (4) religion. The solution to these problems, which are so often intertwined, calls the person into action and thus unfolds the structure of the actualization-process. Each structural facet opens new possibilities for the process of Christianization. Personal actualization must precede Christianization by making the following discoveries:

The discovery of the Ego. (The crystallization of individuality through the correlation of the interior and the exterior, that is, the formation of authenticity.)
The discovery of the Thou. (Formation of the relationship to the Thou of the other sex.)
The discovery of the We. (Formation of relationships and proving oneself in various forms of community life as well as in the encounter with one's fellows as a member of a community.)
The discovery of God. (Formation of a relationship to the numinous, the divine, and, in Christian view, to the God whom Jesus calls His Father.) The path of our thinking begins with psychological phenomena, but it broadens out through association with philosophical reflections into the findings of anthropology. Confronting these with Revelation we work out the points of contact on which pastoral theology can base a theory of pastoral care.

2.

The first task, the discovery of the Ego, stems from the difference and peculiarity of each individual. To work out one's individuality means to seek the authenticity of one's own nature and to authentically experience the significance of one's own existence. This basic experience of the significance of one's own existence, which modern man finds difficult to surmount, leads to two consequences.

First, he who experiences *himself* sees the reality of the inner world in clear confrontation to the reality of the outer world, distinctly separated, each one with its own right-of-existence and alternatively subordinated to the other. In a child the Ego is more or less identified with his environment, and, in accordance with his experience, is fitted into the world as a whole. When the child is rejected and treated with hostility, he suddenly experiences himself as isolated and as confronting a world outside himself. Left on his own, dependent on himself, he is then forced to focus on the inner world, to be rooted in it and to search for its significance. To the degree that he finds his Ego, he experiences this inner world as valuable and grasps the autonomy of the spirit. Then the significance of individual existence is actuated, while the outer world is dismissed into a distance, into a vis-à-vis, able to be formed, but also subordinated. The reality of this experience of the inner world regulates the distance from the outer world and gives it its proper place in a philosophy of life. The right Ego-It relationship is the fruit of the discovery of the Ego. The preponderant technological aspects in the experience of reality, which today affects the child's earliest perceptions, can be corrected only by a strengthening of the inner world. Here in the foreground of individuation, where the values of the outer and inner world are established, is the place of the preliminary decisions regarding a religious attitude. The Gospel asks for an individual attitude toward the outer world, clearly differentiated from one's environment. This can be acquired only when the significance of existence is experienced in one's own inner world.

The second consequence of this necessary experience is to set up the conditions for encounter with men and also with God. In order to carry on a true conversation, one must first be *someone,* and by this we mean, not exteriorly but interiorly. To have found oneself, to have learned to take a stand in one's *self*, to know oneself, to be at home in one's own inner world, to agree with one's own existence—all this amounts to experiencing one's own worth as the right-of-existence. Whoever takes this stand within himself can also confront another: he is *someone*. He does not drift away from the other, but stands firm as himself and endures the tension of encounter. He is capable of conversation. The ability to stand behind one's own existence is the beginning of conversation with another, also with God.

Holy Scripture describes man's position before God in two extreme terms, "worm" (see Job 25:6, Psalms 22:7) and "offspring of God" (Acts 17:29, II Pet. 1:41, Acts 18:29). One hardly dares to think of the latter term, or does such terminology play much of a role in Christian education. The former, however, is used frequently in the teaching about prayer, in ascetics, in the practice of confession, in many sermons and books. Consciousness is surfeited with unworthiness and sinfulness before God. True, the catechetical emphasis on the sonship of God speaks of confidence in Him and of loving dedication, but Christian education tends to obscure the one who is to dedicate himself in love and confidence. Therefore, before he can become *somebody* and find himself, he has been placed in a spiritual cold storage that no longer permits him to say yes to his own nature and to become who he is.[1] As a result he is underdeveloped, unable to hold his own in conversation and, consequently, unable to give God a creative response. He is the one who takes orders, who has to be led.

Of course, even everyday conversation with God has many modulations, and certain situations evoke rather extreme expressions depending on one's character and the peculiarity of the occasion.[2] But in order to communicate with one's Creator in this fashion, it is first of all necessary to be *someone*. He who can truly say "Before God I really feel like a worm that is trodden upon and turns" knows who he is; and his expres-

---

[1] Cf. Pindar: "Become who you are."
[2] In the psalms we find strong personalities who represent a wide scope of human expression toward God.

sion is not merely a mimicry but the outcry of his whole being. In order to be able to bow down, one must first be able to stand straight; in order to be able to converse with another, one must first have his own countenance; in order to be capable of daily conversation with God, one must first be able to stand within oneself and at least have some idea of the significance of one's own existence. In theology, this self-identity is formulated as the *right-of-existence before God*.[3] It is based on the fact of being-created, but only by finding one's own individuality does it permeate consciousness and become experienced as a basis, or underlying current, in one's relationship to God. Pastoral care should, therefore, avoid whatever hinders the formation of individuality, and should positively make individuality and its right-of-existence the starting points of a relationship to God.

3.

The following example will illustrate that human individuality does not unfold and grow as simply and instinctively as, for instance, a plant, but that it is plastic, can be influenced by one's own actions and can be transformed or malformed.

A newcomer is about to come. I am in the group of people awaiting his arrival, and we are alerted to be wary of him: there seems to be something strange about him, something undefined, some dark area in his life. Offhand I attempt to read his face, and what I see in it confirms my suspicions. Then we begin to converse, and he tells me what actually has happened to him. And now his face seems changed, or perhaps it is I who suddenly see him in a new light. His face is expressing something completely different. Was I blind that I could not see this when I first looked at him? What was the obstacle separating me from reality? It was my introjected prejudice, that is, something spiritual, something in the heart that also

---

[3] To avoid misunderstandings we might mention here that this statement is in tension with the *need of salvation*. See Chap. IX in this book.

affected the eye. Human sight is not a mechanical process like that of a camera lens. The eye is connected with everything within me. Prejudice affects the eye, for seeing begins in the heart; and the same holds for hearing, and so forth. The senses do not make objective contact with the outer world; their relationship to it is relative, related to the spiritual contents within me. And just as the senses are plastic, so, too, is my entire nature. I become what I think.[4] The first conscious experience of the relativity of our perception of the external world can have the effect of a shock. It not only brings the peculiarity and plasticity of human material into the immediacy of experience, but also makes us aware that the development of a human being is dependent on his acquired attitudes and dispositions. This is at the same time an opportunity and a risk. Dependence on a certain philosophy, for instance, can so influence a man's relationship to the world that all his perceptions are directed by it. A philosophy thus proves itself, and so the many ideological orientations are not mere possibilities but actually do sweep man into their wake. Centuries-old collective attitudes toward the world (for instance in medieval Europe) mold entire generations; new revolutionary ideas (as, for instance, the scientific thinking of the enlightenment) cause transformations that make previous conceptions of the world obsolete, and no dramatic defense of restoration can undo the change. Man is plastic. He represents a unity of interior and exterior. What is within him determines his relationship to the outer world.

In the spiritual life the effect of this relativity is felt even more. The step toward faith, on man's part, involves his entire life. He must first be open to Revelation and then in turn allow himself to be changed by it. That final step toward

---

[4] We disregard here the fact that this plasticity is limited by one's disposition, especially where there is a considerable deficiency or strong vitality in certain areas, since here we are trying to grasp the phenomenon of plasticity as such.

faith, however, is often prevented by a secret fear that the truth of faith might possibly change his own nature and malform his individuality. He would like to step outside of himself, in order to watch this process of change critically and objectively. The fact is, nevertheless, that the "watcher" has to be involved in the change, with the hope that in accepting the risk of truth his individuality will be confirmed. Now it might be well to first mark off a field where individuality can find itself, in order to pave the way for certain viewpoints to be applied to religious education.

4.

Professional life puts its stamp on human appearance and behavior to such a degree that radically different individuals react in the same way, and that many prove to be only wearers of uniforms rather than their own selves. A teacher, for instance, facing his class alone for the first time, experiences a strange feeling. He must play a role in front of his students and put his heart into it. He knows more than the students; they are the ones to be taught. He must constantly observe the effects of his words and actions on the group in his charge. His position gives him authority and power. The prestige of the teacher, which is keenly felt by the beginner, strengthens the sense of his own worth. However, should he become accustomed to this type of prestige, he may become proud and may develop a self-complacency; hence, he begins to identify with it so that the differentiation of his character from the professional role disappears. Gradually his entire behavior puts on the teacher. Power and authority are then no longer merely a loan; he himself is their embodiment. His self-worth inflates. As husband, as father, as entire man he never forsakes the role of the teacher. At home he directs all conversation; he asks of his family pointed questions and expects the right answers, without the slightest awareness that he is "schoolmastering" everybody and everything.

Psychologically, what has happened here? The profession of the teacher demands that a professional role be played as perfectly as possible for the benefit of students. But instead of leaving his professional garb at school and becoming an ordinary person again, a human being according to his nature, he fuses with his professional role and becomes identified with the prestige of the official person. He reacts to every call as the educator and schoolmaster. He does not realize he is playing a role wherein he is completely absorbed, which he now wears constantly before his face like a mask.[5] The humanness that should outweigh his role-playing is unfortunately squeezed into a professional corset. This humanness can no longer freely develop. Whatever is not commensurate with his professional behavior is excluded from consciousness and repressed. Whatever disturbs a pre-established order; unclear formulations; the deep dark springs of creative energies—all this is denied a place in his life. In other words, he excludes life's fullness.

All professions that have a wide scope of influence seem to embody that strong temptation for one to identify himself with the profession. For the most part such groups are associated with wearing uniforms: military personnel, clergy, academicians, and so forth. The white coat of the physician, for instance, greatly elevates the human position of its wearer—particularly since he is at all times connected with a situation of helping and healing. (Going beyond one's competence in vital questions is always a symptom of the mask.)

In the context of pastoral care, the prime question is, of course, the mask of the pastor. The prestige of the pastoral office is enhanced by the fact that people tend to put the wearer of priestly garb on a pedestal and expect him to respond to it

---

[5] One can compare this invisible mask with the "persona," which the antique actor holds before his face and through which he sounds "personat." C. G. Jung, therefore, calls this mask the *persona*. This psychological *persona* must be clearly differentiated from the philosophical concept of the person.

with piety. Pride, or even more, inner unfulfillment, can fabricate his professional power into a stiff, brocaded vestment that he is not too eager to shed. Once he gets into it, he identifies himself with it. Inevitably his human behavior undergoes a process of change, until finally he can communicate with his flock only through a mask. In spite of his outward zeal and effort, his spiritual appeal lacks something: his message is not carried by his individuality, nor are his words filled with the true power of witness, for he himself does not stand behind them. He is not present. The mask preaches, not he. Later we shall treat more fully the consequences of the priestly mask upon pastoral care.

In education, too, we find the possibility of developing a mask. A father, for example, could not become a lawyer, since his financial situation denied him the opportunity. He suffered this deprivation all his life. His son, of course, will never experience this, for the father is determined to provide him with every opportunity to become a lawyer and attain what he, the father, considers the height of fulfillment in life. Thus he guides his child from his earliest years toward a career in law, without ever questioning whether his son has such aptitude or interest. The son is thus forced to live the life of the father, an alien life. In his tender years his Ego already has alien features: a facade is pasted on, and the unfolding of individuality is hindered. Oppressive educators, proud mothers and ambitious fathers, also directors of boarding schools—these tend to produce such children who lack spontaneity and forwardness, and who leave on others a watered-down, washed-out impression. Often these young people suffer from an overexposed consciousness, a consequence of their association with such adults, and wear a mask without knowing it. For them education has erected a facade behind which their real selves live unconsciously. When the milieu changes, the more vigorous ones will break through the facade, but only to find themselves bewildered and ungrounded. This happens quite frequently when children leave a boarding school, or move into an environment where their religion represents a minority. The more sensitive ones are caught up in the conflict between authority and the self. It is necessary, therefore, that we seek the kind of atmosphere in education that will leave room for guidance and for individual development as well.

A third likely way to form a mask is in the area of so-called public opinion. Hardly anyone can completely avoid its influence. Take advertising for instance: we buy what everyone else buys. This "everyone-does-it world" influences us to buy the clothes everyone is wearing, to read the book everyone is talking about and talk about it the way everyone else does, and to think the way everyone thinks. To the degree that we are influenced by this impersonal, anonymous power of public opinion we wear alien features and, even more so, if we are unconscious of it. We adopt what others feel, think and do. This is as true of the conservative ("it has always been done that way") as it is of the one addicted to progress. In any case one adopts an attitude before one is able to react authentically. One does not think and decide for oneself; the power of decision is not even called upon. The person who alone is capable to decide is not yet actualized, still lies dormant and sinks back into potential existence. In politics, as well, propaganda and advertising help to capitalize on the mask-forming effect of public opinion. These political methods are antipersonal, and the end products are not individuals but rather standardized collective existences who are obedient executive organs of that anonymous power, publicity.

Public opinion is found also in the Church: in a parish, perhaps, a standardized judgment about a person makes the rounds; a youth group develops an exclusive spiritual *esprit de corps;* a sermon is constructed with all the techniques of mass-communication—it does not address the individual, does not call forth a personal response but tries to persuade with threats and promises, with skillful play upon the emotions.

The outcome is a religious mask. But this is not the fruit of competent pastoral care ʻ orientated toward the Gospel of Christ.

The fourth tendency toward mask-formation is self-education. And this produces the most dangerous kind of mask. Since living in society would end in catastrophe if everyone behaved as a crude, uncultured product of nature, we must all undergo changes within ourselves, must guide, refine and educate ourselves. To live with oneself is to work on oneself. Weaknesses, failures and unpleasant dispositions must be eradicated. In religious-life circles, where examination of conscience, ascetical practices and striving for perfection are stressed as ways of self-improvement, the imitation of an ideal is often recommended. A very exact way of life is thus constructed, including the control of each day—so exact that it obstructs the development of one's nature. On the other hand, who can prove that a self-devised *ideal* is in line with the *idea*[6] inherent in man, the idea God had of him when He created him? It is quite possible then that the self-made ideal can endanger the development of the Creator's idea, for the natural growth of an individual cannot be calculated or determined in advance, especially when we consider the long journey through the age-levels.[7] Self-education can produce a pseudo personality that contradicts the very nature of man. This is certainly the case when, after a year-long striving to attain a mistaken ideal, the outcome is a way of life contrary to the structural laws of the individual, that is, contrary to nature's way of development. Such a human being lives in opposition to his own nature. He misses his own truth, his own being—he wears a mask. The man behind the mask can be described as follows: he excludes life's fullness; he leads an alien life; he avoids personal decisions; he bypasses his nature. The discrep-

[6] Cf. H. E. Hengstenberg, *Askese als Mittel Göttlicher Vorsehung und Führung* (Würzburg, 1940).
[7] See Chap. XI in this book.

ancy between the exterior and interior, between appearance and content makes this man unauthentic. Both inside and outside the effects are obvious. The mask acts as an intervening layer breaking down the relationship to the outer world. The man behind the mask sees the external world through colored glasses of various hues and no longer sees reality as it is. Such a man is biased toward his outer world. His difficulties in social life, with colleagues, neighbors, superiors and subjects, are not based on conscious mistakes but rooted in the unconscious. In spite of his conscious efforts, his relationship to the outer world is always distorted; it is affected by the mask.

Behind these symptoms is a fact of universal significance: the human psyche influences one's relationship to the outer world, a relationship not at all static as the distance between two houses, but relative, that is, subject to everything existing in man. Every look at the world is under the selecting influence of the inner realm, and the world-concept becomes relative, becomes a subjective world-design. Thus every mask causes such a one-sided world-design. This fact is of special interest for the pastor, since in his endeavor to convert men he not only deals with their thoughts and opinions, but also comes in contact with their world-design—for conversion means to change that image.

But likewise the pastor's mask forms a world-design. In that case he no longer sees the Gospel realistically, but merely through the selective medium of his subjectivity. Equally hidden from him is the full reality of his parish, for he sees only what his mask permits. It blocks a truly Christian view of the world and thus impairs the realization of faith. Faith, however, penetrates the world-design, helps bring it closer to truth and thus replaces its subjective character with an objective view of the world: world as creation, corresponding to a certain phase of salvation history. But the influence of faith must go beyond the level of intellect, of mere thought, for just as a mask succeeds in subtly deceiving the senses, faith, too, permeates the senses, the relationship with fellow man, as well as the entire world-design, assimilating it to reality. Imperceptibly, the believer comes to see his environment in its true co-ordination; he is able to judge it correctly, which in turn strengthens his faith. Realization of faith and freedom from the mask have a reciprocal effect.

The effects of a mask are even more damaging to his internal world. The man behind the mask does not live the fullness, the very core of his being. He does not live his *self;* rather he is lived. He is not grounded in his *self,* is not himself, is not completely there, and he does not fully *exist.*

His individuality is not merely covered up, but not even present, not there yet. The one living there is a somebody in disguise, one who has formed a false body[8] and one whose appearance is distorted. He then could and should be different, corresponding to his intrinsic self; but this was not yet called to life; its generative power has been blocked or even led astray. Spatially and biologically, he is there, in the sense of being materially "present," but he is not present as he who exists in act. He did not come to grips with his existence, and as the existentialists would say, he is not existent.[9] As a result he cannot understand himself; his existential insight is submerged as if in a fog. His *self* is not activated; he does not act as himself.

A common symptom of such an individual is his abnormal need of self-assurance,[10] which is manifested in his constant

[8] Often enough, this takes revenge through neurotic symptoms.

[9] Cf. Martin Heidegger's interpretation of "man." The world of the impersonal "one" prevents man from penetrating into his existence. He is only "extant," not in-the-world, not existent. Jasper's corresponding terms are: authenticity, unauthenticity.

[10] Robust individuals come to a standstill at the turning point of their life, at about 40; they begin, resignedly, to mark time. More differentiated natures, however, experience a "void" and meaninglessness in their life and often escape into neurotic symptoms. These should be recognized as a call for authenticity and for life-significance, which could be found in the formation of individuality.

search for excessive external activity. This inner insecurity is especially evident in his spiritual life, which here too takes the form of excessive external activity. Since he fears to stand empty-handed before God, he must look for some *thing*: some accomplishment, some good works, or an exaggerated fidelity to the law so as to prove his worth. In order to distract God from seeing his real self, he puts on a show of achievement and of observing all sorts of proprieties even before the question of guilt and atonement presents itself—as if it were wrong for him to exist at all. That which in the secular area is experienced as the absurdity of life, in the spiritual area manifests itself as being at fault.[11]

5.

Yet, the experience of the significance of one's own existence is the fruit of a firm stand within oneself, of a truly formed individuality. In the area of religion, this means to become unfolded as the Creator's idea, and to accept the fact that he was created. But since this can be experienced in life only to the degree that individuality has been achieved, pastors and educators are faced with the problem of the urgent need to help others toward its fulfillment. There is a great need for the formation of an educational climate favorable to the growth of individuality. All conditions that lead to the formation of a mask should be consciously avoided, and all doors swung open to the fullness of life, in order to facilitate the discovery of one's own life. The capacity for decision needs to be systematically called forth, and one's own truth developed. Innate unfolding must be coupled with conscious formation and independence with guidance. Such an educational atmosphere can be created if the laws of polarity are respected.

[11] This "being-at-fault" must be clearly distinguished from guilt and sin based on conscious decision and action. "Being-at-fault" is something purely psychological; it is in the religious foreground and should be corrected before a dialogue with God can begin.

Electricity gives the most lucid idea of polarity. Two poles are in tension with each other: the one positive, the other negative. One by itself is powerless; only the uniting current can produce an effect. The current oscillates between the two poles and light flares up. All of life seems to be structured according to this model.[12] Forces oscillate and fluctuate between two poles and in the middle of them life comes forth. The same holds true for the educational sphere: the potential of each pole should be activated so that the current can cause life. More concretely stated, this means: The forces of the pupil and the forces of the educator should collide and, if a true polarity occurs, there will in fact be growth in each one's individuality; in other words, the unfolding of human nature comes into tension with the demands of education, of community, of the teacher, so that it can produce the individual man. In the area of religious education and pastoral care, this interaction of poles follows this procedure: human nature, as one of the two poles, comes into tension with God's call and His Revelation. Of course, only an actualized, individual human nature could be the fully effective pole to God's Word. Through the alternating current between the two poles light and faith come forth.

The *personal* effectiveness of spiritual polarities, however, cannot be grasped from an example of physics. Such a tension is not a comfortable situation but implies a constant unrest that has to be mastered. The polarity of masculine-feminine, for instance, runs through the entire world of man. To avoid it means to remain sterile, biologically and even more so spiritually, for the entire cosmos bears masculine and feminine features. The unrelenting tension between these poles demands discussion and constant decision. Therefore, polaric tension offers the opportunity for decisions, calls to the deciding authority, the *person*. This aspect of polarity is most important

[12] Cf. Romano Guardini, *Der Gegensatz* (Mainz, 1955).

in pastoral care, since incarnation of divine life is possible only on the *personal* level. Emphasis on the laws of polarity is therefore a prerequisite for a solid foundation of pastoral care and education.

a) The first law of polarity is *action-reaction.* Two poles are connected with each other, the same as two scales of a balance. Every change on one side effects a counteraction on the other. The law of action and reaction binds both poles. If, for instance, one side is weighted down with an overly feminine, mother-dominated education, the other side hangs impotent in the air. The result will be a lack of confidence in the outer world, a situation that could have been counterbalanced by the contribution of a genuine father. On the other hand, an overload of the demanding, oppressive father will stunt the growth of a healthy sense of self-worth, which condition might have developed in the warm, loving care of the true mother.

This type of inferiority can also be very easily developed in spiritual life, since Christianity, along with Judaism and Islamism, seems to be a masculine religion. The God of the Christians shows a masculine countenance to man, in all three Persons. Consequently, the masculine aspect is acknowledged and cultivated, while the feminine aspect is ordinarily expressed in naive sentiments, prayers, hymns and even pictures to match. Thus the educational atmosphere in religion as well ought to be influenced by the masculine-feminine polarity, so that the fullness of life can enter. The first law of polarity is action-reaction.

b) The second law of polarity, *tension,* is caused by fluctuation between the poles. There is a constant up-and-down motion, a to-and-fro, between the poles, similar to the tension of current oscillating between the poles of an electric light bulb. This means that polarities are constantly in tension, a fact that can be experienced in the outer world of ever changing situations, and in the inner world of ever present unrest over its continuous problems. Consequently, there is no rest for the educator in this type of educational atmosphere.

c) The energy flows from the farthest point of one pole toward the other, and in the center, where they collide, the sparking takes place. Every educator tries to find the middle ground, the equilibrium between guidance and self-determination that leads to at least a temporary balance. We cannot aim at a fusion of the poles—authority and freedom, for instance, do not fuse—but it is possible to steer the tension in such way that there is such temporary balance. For the pupil the happy times of balance are his productive hours. He is, as it were, absorbed by the healthy tension of being assisted and that of being left to his own resources in a kind of balancing act. And it may well be that this situation awakens in him a delight in his own decision-making. Then the youngster is bewildered by this new reality of free decision in his life and sees his individuality clearly differentiated from that of the instructor, whom he accepts and with whom he is basically in agreement. The student feels a strange new empathy with his instructor, which gives him courage to appropriate his own uniqueness. The relationship between teacher and student, or superior and subject, changes into a relationship of master-disciple. If this were but so in religious education and life! Thus the third law in the structure of polarity is the search for the center, the equilibrium, the *balance*.

Fidelity to these three laws of polarity in the field of education guarantees life; and neglect of them, be it through weakness, inexperience or anxiety, obstructs life. And proper application of these laws nets the following results:

1. The possibility for growth, for one's own unfolding and self-development is made accessible, thus leading to formation of individuality.

2. The center of man is called forth, the deciding, responsible authority: the *person*. Education according to the laws of polarity is a call to the *person*.

3. The inner world becomes firm and thus sets up a counterbalance against the outer world. The individual is now able to resist the pull of the outer world and is in less danger of becoming absorbed and of losing himself in exterior things. Both the inner and the outer, the I and the it, are experienced as the two pillars of a bridge. In the security of taking his stand in the world, man begins to experience the integration of subject and object. His world-design comes closer to truth, becomes more true.

6.

In the field of religious education and pastoral care, we find three important polarities:

(1) Protection vs. challenge
(2) Habit vs. spontaneity
(3) Past dimension vs. future dimension

(1) The first polarity is *protection vs. challenge*. All young people will clash with their parents, teachers and pastors because they are not permitted this or that. The older generation wants to protect, but the youth rebels: "I want to face challenges on my own. I have to learn to make decisions for myself and can't expect adults to give me all the answers. I have to answer for myself—sure, I'm taking a chance, being on my own, but this is exactly what I want! How can a fellow really find himself if those in authority don't give him a chance to get out and get some experience. I can't simply take the "book" answers in religion—I've got to work my faith out for myself —and I don't think you have to be afraid that I'll lose my faith. If I can't associate with nonbelievers for fear of losing my faith, then it's not worth very much. . . . And if a seminarian can't keep his vocation associating with real people in the world, then I don't think he has one. But the only way to know is to give it the test. . . ." Opposition of this sort is met everywhere, and is frequently found in seminaries and reli-

gious houses of formation. But there the discussions are generally only among the students and for that reason all the more
contagious. Seldom do they find their way to superiors in the
form of an open rebellion. But is this strife of the youth
justified? Has youth not the right to prove itself?

The responsible educator answers: "They know neither the
dangers of the world nor their own strength. The world is so
cunning and tricky, temptation so camouflaged, and religion
so much under the attack of the enemy that even adults go
astray. How much more this holds true for the young who are
generally so naive and whose strength is still developing! It
is only reasonable to establish a reserve, where young life is
protected from too much danger and can find and strengthen
itself for the struggle of life." This viewpoint of the world is
certainly not naive and obliges educators to set up and maintain a realm of protection.

Thus challenge and protection confront each other as do two
poles that hold the educational atmosphere in constant tension. Every action of the one side leads to a reaction on the
other. When protection is overstressed, opposition grows into
passive resistance; but too much freedom again shows irre-
sponsibility, since it overtaxes the strength of the young. Over-
protection in any event creates an educational hothouse. Too
much freedom of decision, on the other hand, burdens the conscience of the educators who might otherwise have saved a
youngster from dangers that are too great for him to cope
with. Both educator and pastor must take into account the law
of action and reaction. They must protect, and yet allow the
challenge of independence. They must accept the tension and
strive for a balance. Their care must be coupled with courage,
and they must put trust in initiative with suggestions as to
how the world can be mastered "on one's own." In short,
polaric education and pastoral care make very definite demands
on educator and pastor. If we put all these demands together

we discover the actual characteristics of the true educator and pastor.[13]

(2) The second polarity is *habit vs. spontaneity*. In religious education this includes: authority vs. freedom; guidance vs. self-determination. Authority and guidance seek to ingrain habits of religious behavior, while freedom and self-determination manifest themselves in spontaneous religious actions.

Everyone knows to what extent habits help to overcome periods of fatigue. It is a blessing that old habits are so rooted in daily life, for this allows nature to take its course without using up extra energy, and thus many necessary actions can be carried out mechanically. Education at home and at school, as well as self-education, aim at this goal. Habits also have an important place in religious formation, especially since it is so difficult to keep religiously alert. Therefore, both the religious life of the home and formal religious education must ingrain habits as lasting supports. The child must become accustomed to Sunday Mass, to receiving the sacraments regularly, to saying his daily prayers. Conscience must be trained to react forcefully to certain actions and omissions. These habits are a scaffolding that help support life; they are like grooves set in the system. What's more, they endure throughout all of life. It is the task of prudent pastoral care to build and maintain such powerful habits that will compel the faithful to fulfill religious obligations.

Moses and Elias are models of successful dealing with people who are weak. "Habits must be burned into their flesh with red-hot tongs."[14] It is not without meaning that these two rigorous religious leaders were present at Christ's transfiguration. The name of God would have long been forgotten were it not for the courageous and far-seeing men who accepted the burden of leadership and responsibility and so came to reli-

[13] See below, pp. 88 ff.
[14] Cf. Peter Lippert, "Moses and Elias Stand Beside Thee," in *Job the Man Speaks with God* (New York, 1936).

gion's rescue. This attitude, so often a temptation for religious leaders, is depicted in its extreme in Dostoevski's Grand Inquisitor. It is worth our while to consider it.

The Grand Inquisitor defends his pastoral viewpoint against Christ and reproaches Him for His errors: "Man should follow Thee freely, enticed and taken captive by Thee . . . man must decide for himself. They could not have been left in greater confusion and suffering. . . . I swear, man is weaker and baser by nature than Thou hast believed him! . . . We have corrected Thy work and have founded it upon miracle, mystery and authority. And men rejoiced that they were again led like sheep. . . . Thou art proud of Thine elect, but Thou hast only the elect, while we give rest to all. . . . Then we shall give them the quiet humble happiness of weak creatures such as they are by nature. . . . In their leisure hours we shall make their life like a child's game, with children's songs and innocent dance. . . . Then I will stand up and point out to Thee the thousand millions of happy children who have known no sin."

This viewpoint of the Grand Inquisitor is shared by men in both politics and religion who believe that they know how to deal with man. Their policy says once again: "Habits must be burned into their flesh with red-hot tongs." We even find attempts for a theological foundation of this viewpoint by alluding to original sin as the cause of man's weakness.

Without a doubt, the Grand Inquisitor represents an extreme, but an extreme that nevertheless points to certain truths. Without the hard and fast traditional customs established by the strict leadership of pastors, and preserved in the same strictness, the process of the elimination of Christian ideas would have progressed much more rapidly in many areas. It is so true that man needs leadership and well-formed habits.

The other side, however, maintains: "A true religious act can be born only out of free decision. Only a spontaneous act is truly religious. A forced prayer is not a prayer, a forced

Sunday Mass is no true worship. True, Moses compelled his people—but Christ does not compel anyone. Christ withstood the temptations to force man into His Kingdom by means of either miracles, magic or political power.[15] In confronting the Pharisee, the spiritual man of His time, Christ stood up against a religion of purely objective law and demanded personal decision. Thus religion is possible only in free choice. Every kind of coercion and habituation must be rejected, for religion without personal viewpoint is contrary to the spirit of the Gospel. Rather, religious education must aim at spontaneous and free religious response." This attitude is also extreme since, according to the law of action and reaction, the other side of the scale is again left hanging in the air inasmuch as man is overloaded. Yet this extreme also points to certain truths: the Gospel asks for an independent, free decision of the individual. And Christianity is a *personal* religion, whereas a religion of pure habit is something mechanical, something pre*personal*.

But why is it that all educators and pastors fail when they appeal only to man's constant and free decision? Why, strange to say, do children become fearful when they are without guidance and left to fend for themselves? Doubtlessly man is a *personal* being and must constantly be called to *personal* acts, but, as experience shows, man cannot maintain the *personal* level, for he is prone to falling back to the pre*personal* level. Every painfully achieved *personal* relationship between humans deteriorates time and time again to the thing-level and must be newly developed. Every religious act, if often repeated, is in danger of becoming a thing. The celebration of the Eucharist, for instance, becomes merely a "thing" to do; *personal* alertness cannot be maintained, even in the love-relationship to God. Thus what originated in spontaneity would disappear completely if habit did not carry it through the tired, empty,

[15] Matt. 4:1–11.

arid periods. Of course, man, when living at the pre*personal* level, does not live up to himself, nor does he fulfill the demands of the Gospel. But it is just as much in the spirit of the Gospel to provide man with help when he is tired and simply overburdened by the constant call to alertness for decision. Hence it is sensible, for example, when one makes it a habit to go to confession every month or every three months, knowing that he needs this help to keep him from becoming indifferent. Many people even need a prepared formula for confession (including a good, catechetically-approved examination of conscience).[16] The same holds true for the habit of daily prayer, since there can be long periods of time when spontaneous prayer is not possible. Habit is like a ladder for climbing up again to the *personal* level—which in any case is certainly easier than starting from scratch to build a new prayer life. Human life moves between the high points of *personal* acts and the low points of pre*personal* habits, and spiritual life flows between genuine *personal* piety and pre*personal* habits.

Thus a religious atmosphere built on the polarity of habit and spontaneity aids the development of the *personally*-weakened man. A *minimum* of habit must be coupled with constant openness for spontaneity; whereas, a *maximum* of habit creates the danger of a mask. A poor formation of habits results in the burden of too much decision-making, while a healthy attempt to balance both poles provides the necessary help and stimulates the spontaneity of individual spiritual life. In other words, such a balance offers individuality in the religious sphere as well.

(3) A third polarity seems to be in order wherever a life in society deals with education, and that is the *dimension of past vs. dimension of future*. To be related to the past means to lean upon traditions, to be rooted in former generations.

---

[16] See Josef Goldbrunner's essay "Zur Beichtspiegelfrage," in *Katechetische Blätter* (July, 1959), pp. 289–291, and "Über die Person und das Personale" (January, 1960), pp. 1–7.

The past burdens us with the works of our forebears, but at the same time renders us the fruit of their labors by enabling us to learn the meaning of human life from previous experiences. A nation's past is as truly mother as is the motherland; both are needed to find roots in the world. Yet, if too much stress is laid on the past, the educational atmosphere oppresses the young and threatens to suffocate all new life. The religious atmosphere, too, is often so much influenced by the dimension of the past that it seems to be its only basis. But, in spite of our reverence for the past, in no way can it be the content of life but merely its point of departure, for life naturally tends forward, not backward. In the home, in educational institutions, in religious instruction, in the Church[17]—in all of these the concept of future dimension must come into productive tension with the dimension of the past. What comes from the past cannot be the only determining factor, since it can be changed in the future. Tradition is nourishment, but not for itself alone—rather for life that must look into the future and seek its own form. Reaching out to the future is a basic gesture of life. Thus the ever changing future, with all its possibilities of change and of the new, must assume its proportionate value in our homes, schools and institutions, as well as in religious instruction and in the Church. These future possibilities must be given their true value both essentially, through orientation to the future, and existentially, through the attitude of educator and pastor. But it must be done skillfully.

Every teacher experiences that the spirit of a class changes with the approach of graduation. The students are no longer completely present; they are, so to speak, swept into the future. In this situation it is understandable that students would leap over the present and be absorbed by the future. But in one's spiritual life this attitude would be a clever way to sneak away

[17] Cf. Josef Goldbrunner, ed., *The Dimension of Future in our Faith* (Notre Dame, 1966).

from life (as stated by Kierkegaard). It would indicate a lack of understanding the Gospel. The Christian must achieve a relationship to the future world that allows for him to stand upright in the present, that enables him to see the present in its proper light and to enjoy it.

An example: Someone expects to undergo serious surgery in a few days. He considers all possibilities and, as a consequence of this consciousness of the future dimension, he will see his fellow men in a different way during the days preceding his operation. He will talk to them with more awareness and confront them more consciously than before. His future dimension does not compete with his present tasks; rather it gives him a new awareness of the present. In Christian proclamation, *future dimension* should always be linked with *hidden presence* so that both can work together.[18]

Education represents an anticipation of the future, as Eduard Spranger says.[19] It is a mixture of desire, a sense for the future and of awaiting. Developmental processes of the past and present are extended, as probabilities, into the future. One takes into account unexpected events, both positive and negative, and one awaits in fear and confidence. The courage to risk uncertainty is aroused, and through ascesis and training one is strengthened to endure and wait. It is not purely incidental that science fiction is so much in demand, and that a writer like Teilhard de Chardin is so popular.[20] As one who is inspired by the future, he radiates "confidence in the great development of being."[21] "To be one with this unfolding"[22] is his favorite expression. Chardin gives finality the precedence

[18] See above, pp. 47 ff.
[19] Cf. Eduard Spranger, *Pädagogische Perspektiven* (Heidelberg, 1962), II.
[20] In this context we are interested only in his attitude toward the future, which, however, seems to be an essential attraction of his books.
[21] Cf. Teilhard de Chardin, *Letters from a Traveller* (New York, 1962).
[22] *Ibid.*

over causality in both the world and in human life.

Unfortunately, our proclamation of the Gospel is often insufficiently molded by the eschatological teaching of the future. Yet all of Holy Scripture breathes the future dimension of Jesus. In the Christian world-concept, however, finality is unimportant in comparison to causality, the doctrine of creation, the fall of man, and redemption. Yet only eschatology, the proclamation of the full Revelation of God's kingship over the world, gives the decision of faith and religious life their full meaning. The finality of the Christian world-concept corresponds to the ultimate striving of the human psyche; it could become a sustaining power of the life of faith, if the dimension of future would find its proper place in the realm of education and pastoral care.

Hence, educators and pastors who are inspired by the future are of much more value than those who still look to the past. They add to every educational field an element having the effect of a liberating and stimulating medicine. They put children and adolescents unconsciously in touch with the future. In the religious field we have two characteristics of the between-time, namely the dimension of future in eschatology and the hidden presence of the future, which are an added help for a conscious relationship to the future.

7.

Such polaric structure is effective in a threefold way.

a) It calls to self-development, demanding but protecting and helping, a call that provides a respite for gaining new strength. It offers the possibility of finding oneself: one's true life can fully develop; one can learn to live one's own life. The capacity of decision is activated and one's own truth is experienced.

Concisely, this educational endeavor should make it possible for me as a person to find my individuality. My inner world finds its ground as I experience myself—sense my true

being, my being-I—as a unit closed within itself and yet able
to open itself up. To live my own true being, pure and without
interference, permits a contact with the self that allows me not
only to accept myself but also to agree with myself. *Omne ens
est bonum,* "every being is good." When this scholastic axiom
is experienced in my own inner world, it brings significance
to my own existence. "My being is good," and I can also say
"It is important that I exist." The formation of my individuality, as a first step toward the actualization of my *person,*
reveals in living experience, that is, existentially, a structural
facet: the significance of my unique existence.

b) Through this development, the individual's inner world
is not only anchored in itself, but it is also able to withstand
the impact of the outer world. Even more, it forms the necessary counterweight against the outer world, which is recognized as only half of the total reality. Thus both halves form
an individual world-design, in which inner and outer world
are integrated. The taking a stand in the world comprises the
inner and the outer realm.

c) Applied to religion, to sense one's own individual being
means to touch the ground where God has put man: "I want
you to exist!" The idea of creatureliness is realized; thus I know
that I am wanted; I touch the act of creation within myself and
experience myself as intended—God consents to my existence.
To comprehend all this in a peculiar, often presentient and
yet realistic, experience means to understand one's right-of-
existence before God!

Doubtlessly, there is danger here, for everyone knows how
easily such consciousness of the self can turn into arrogant
independence. Therefore the right-of-existence before God
must be coupled with another, equally existential, experience
—the need of salvation.[23] But a negative fear of danger should
not obstruct the positive interpretation, namely, that the exis-

[23] See below, p. 118.

tential experience of one's right-of-existence before God is the prerequisite for partnership with Him. One who has no solid foothold in himself stumbles clumsily in a conversation with a superior human being, or else overcompensates with arrogance. Never does it lead to a conversation on the same level, free and open to all the possibilities of give and take that make for creative conversation. This is all the more important in regard to God. An underdeveloped individuality, which prevents the experience of the significance of one's own existence, is often the primary reason why the partnership with God, one that He himself promises and so greatly desires, cannot be realized.

But once this partnership is more or less understood, there is, previous to and independent of any guilt, the possibility to meet God face to face, as a partner, as a Thou, as a person. What was experienced previously as a divine Being now becomes a real partner for conversation who permits, seeks and awaits a relationship; hence, the actuality of an individual relationship to God can now be realized.

Evidently, the idea of guilt is no longer the same. The immature assault against a God who hides behind morality, the Church and ethical imperatives is transformed into a mature, fully responsible approach toward Him, since this is the obvious consequence when a man can meet God as a partner.

Sermons, lectures or catechetics will never bring such a relationship to fruition, for it can develop only through the formation of a structure of polarities. This is the problem that must be faced by the educator and the pastor himself.

8.

The difficulty of creating an educational sphere structured by polarities becomes obvious when we contrast it to other existent structures. There is the *either/or* attitude, which defends only the one side, for instance, it advocates *only* protection or *only* challenge but cannot adjust to a middle way.

It is a much simpler method and gives the impression of strict justice; but instead of providing help for the development of individuality, it is based on authoritative control that is mechanically manipulated, without consideration for the various stages of maturing. Controversial questions either dare not raise their head, or else are dealt with in an impersonal, indeed autocratic, way. The educator replaces human kindness with the simplifying function of a supervisor.

The opposite extreme is the *as-well-as* attitude. In the guise of broadmindedness this attitude consents to every impulse with the same intensity. It avoids decision and benevolently agrees with both sides—an attitude not only indicating lack of leadership but also creating a relativistic leveling tendency. Hidden behind a facade of broadmindedness often lies a kind of resigned skepticism. But the educator himself must actively determine values and live them as inspiring example.

On the other hand, education based on polarities cannot develop with a one-sided educator who eliminates the other side by use of his authority. It needs one who sees both sides, not merely equalizing and playing off one side against the other, but rather creating a fertile tension. He cannot take a seat on one side; he must be constantly in motion, flexible and aware that the new life of those entrusted to him can develop and find itself only through a never ceasing discussion. He is not an equalizer but a correlator; not a mechanical, calculating correlator, but one who creates possibilities, calls, appeals, helps, supports, yet never forces. Symbol of his educational attitude is not a high encircling fence or a concrete wall, but the inviting open door of his house.

Certainly he faces the risk that one of those entrusted to him might leave without returning, and thus will be lost. Dismayed and surprised, and not without compassion, he faces the impenetrable fact that a youngster has turned away in spite of the excellent educational and pastoral conditions provided for him. Should he have locked the door? Should he have contradicted the laws of polarity, yielding to the *either/or* viewpoint?

Locked doors and high fences do not guarantee a successful education. Parents of great piety often see their adolescent child deciding against faith, without being able to force a change in his attitude. Education based on polarities confronts the educator with this possibility—and it takes courage to cope with it. Polarities stabilize the critical point in that they call for the development of individuality and free decision. Isn't this taking too much of a risk? Great is the temptation to play Providence and at times give a little push. But the task of religious education and pastoral care is to stand by and offer help in situations where human endeavor touches the dividing line between salvation and damnation. Whoever creates a polaric structure must be able to endure this existential depth where yawns the abyss of irrevocable events. Its fruit will be a grasp of wisdom—but only the beginning of wisdom. For one who experiences the preciousness of human existence, sensing it in the significance of his own being, will love human nature and find his delight in calling the young to meet the challenge of individuality.

CHAPTER VIII

Capacity for Encounter and Partnership with God

1.

A PERSON with developed individuality does not necessarily open up to partnership and let the *I* find the way to the *Thou*. An individual may live side by side for many years with his fellow men without actually meeting them. He is withdrawn into himself, and his relationships to the outer world are merely on the intellectual, volitional or emotional level, merely tactical and without *personal* involvement. This noncommittal attitude can be found among neighbors, colleagues and even between married people.[1] A pastor, too, can be separated from his community in such way that the faithful remain merely the object of his generally ultracorrect pastoral efforts. He has found no personal relationship with them. His capacity for encounter has remained undeveloped, traumatized or perhaps worn thin through discouragement, defiance or resignation. Likewise, one may live a very pious life and use

[1] Cf. Ibsen, *A Doll's House* (Boston, 1890), and the film *Wild Strawberries* by Ingmar Bergman.

God only as the confirmation of one's correctness. He has never encountered God Himself.

Individuality must undergo a process of opening up, not by force but spontaneously. It should abandon the monologue and enter the dialogue, not in a mere exchange of thoughts but in a readiness for confrontation. Inner self-development should awaken and cultivate the capacity for encounter. This process of spontaneous opening will activate another structural facet of the person, his *dialogical mode of being,* for he is created for dialogue and for opening up to the Thou. The practice of human encounter is the first step toward the difficult encounter with an invisible vis-à-vis, with God, since only human encounter makes possible the realization of an encounter with God.

Human beings meet one another in many ways, but encounter between the sexes, in which the I is confronted with the Thou, has a special power to awaken the capacity for encounter. This psychic development affects all other forms of encounter. It has unchallengeable persuasiveness in calling the person to open up, thus perfectly exemplifying the penetration through the psychic into the *personal* sphere.

Its effect is intensified by the impetus of a strong biological and spiritual power—love. Before we attempt to unfold the entire complex procedure from outside to inside, it is necessary to first clarify terms and to avoid misinterpretations.

a) Primarily, let us consider three aspects of the meaning of love:

Love

Sex   Eros   Agape

Sex is the physical power of love, a bodily energy that differentiates the sexes. It includes instincts, drives and the organs of reproduction.

Eros is the psychic and spiritual power of love, the capacity for loving relationships with persons, things and situations (for instance, one's place of work). Eros loves what is good, true and beautiful; it is orientated to the realm of values.

Seen together, Sexus and Eros are like the upper and lower sides of natural human love. It is our task to form and cultivate this kind of love, since it is the material from which the capacity for encounter develops.

God's way and kind of love is *Agape*. It is supernatural love, first revealed to us by God (I John 4:7–10) and then given us as grace in baptism. It is a task of Christian life to allow this gift to "become flesh," that is, to incarnate it by transforming natural love and allowing it to become converted into *Agape*—the same as the intellect, will and emotions surrender to the grace of faith, allowing the believer to begin thinking like Christ.[2] Human love, therefore, is the natural basis for *Agape*.[3] But it is transformed through the incarnation of the gift of grace, and this transformation is part of the conversion process. Its fruit is the capacity for encounter with God. The more the person makes use of the power of love, forming it in a personal way, the more plastic will it become for the incarnation of divine love in *Agape*.

b) Human love is a complexity, the levels of which can be analyzed separately; nevertheless it should be viewed as a unity. Failure to see human love in this context is a frequent source of misunderstandings and lopsided attitudes that can lead to biological, emotional and even religious fixations, often detrimental to the development of faith. Since taboos frequently block a clear view in this area, it is fitting to use the following illustration of the complex unity of human love.

The question "What is a pearl" can be answered from many different aspects. The chemist tells us that it is a carbide, and the biologist that it is an abnormal growth of a mollusk. The

[2] Cf. Thaddaeus Soiron, *Glaube, Hoffnung, Liebe* (Leipzig und Regensburg, 1934), p. 34.

[3] "Gratia supponit naturam, non destruit sed elevat."

merchant sees a pearl as an object to sell, whereas to a woman it is a precious ornament. The poet again sees the pearl as a "tear of the sea." Of course, every one is right, since the truth about the pearl is manifold and comprises all those answers. Whoever excludes one aspect, thinking it profane—for instance, accepting the chemical or biological viewpoint—fails to do justice to the truth and, even more, divests himself of effective aids, for the chemist can tell him exactly what kind of acid will destroy the pearl.

The same applies to human love. It has many aspects, and only he who sees all its levels, and is willing to accept them, will approach a full understanding. Again we must rely on biology, philosophy, theology, and, last but not least, depth psychology to help us see the whole truth. To stay within the pastoral-theological viewpoint, we shall work in the immediacy of experience.

2.

From the biological viewpoint, we can comprehend merely the urge of the sexes toward each other for the purpose of coitus and reproduction. This level, called Sex, is a physiological love based on sexual differentiation. By way of expert instruction suited to the developmental stage of the individual, it is the educator's task, and that of religious education as well, to smooth the way for the awakening of Sexus during puberty, and to offer understanding help, so that Sexus may find its proper place in a Christian way of life. Instruction in the physiology of sex should begin with the child's first questions about motherhood and should continue until he is ready for marriage. Any lack of clarification obstructs the *personal* permeation of Sexus. It is also imperative that the introduction of sexual knowledge take into account the psychological fact of the *psychic* barrier against incest, which must not be broken down. This holds especially for discussions about fatherhood. It means that consanguinity and close relationship often make it very difficult, or even impossible, to discuss subjects of the intimate sphere of Sex. Sexual instruction, consequently, should be the task of teachers, catechists and youth counselors, rather than of the parents.[4]

"Christian ascetics" must make it clear that "man is . . . doing well as long as he is aware of his urges, including his immoral tendencies and endures the pain of their conscious integration. This suffering at the same time aids the preservation of spiritual and physical health."[5] In other words, in any encounter between the sexes sex will be involved either as an underground current or an open one on the surface. Consciously or unconsciously it will be active.

3.

On the borderline between Sexus and Eros is a law that prevails through the entire cosmos: the law of attraction and repulsion. It rules the stars and the minerals; also it is the reason why many plants are unable to grow side by side. Animals are united and separated by it. Man, too, is affected by it,[6] perceiving it psycho-physiologically more or less clearly as a kind of scent. The more that experience and self-awareness bring this barometric reaction into consciousness, the more man is able to deal with the problem resulting from this law. This means that in his life in society he can govern sympathy and antipathy—terms corresponding to attraction and repulsion on the human level—from an objective point of view.

Sympathy or antipathy can be in evidence even before a

[4] It is difficult to discuss the intimate sphere when strong emotional ties interfere. This applies to both parents and children. A human distance is necessary in order to speak objectively about the intimate sphere of the sexual. Cf. Friedrich Schneider, *Katholische Familienerziehung* (Freiburg, 1961), pp. 277 ff.

[5] Cf. Hans Eduard Hengstenberg, *Christliche Askese* (Regensburg, 1936), p. 93; see also Bernhard Stöckle, *Gottgesegneter Eros* (Ettal, 1962).

[6] Cf. Goethe, *Elective Affinities* (New York, 1885).

single word has been uttered to the other. It is an intuitive reaction of our own body-soul union to the particular nature of the other—a manifestation that often shocks, seldom deceives and, even more seldom, accepts correction. In the sexual encounter, these spontaneous reactions play either a dividing or a uniting role between Sexus and Eros, and because the momentum of these reactions later on determines the mutual level of affect,[7] they should be given all the more attention when an encounter is to be maintained and led into a community of marriage and family.

Antipathy, if not brought to awareness and controlled, can be the cause of much misunderstanding and misguided behavior. The other person can either do or neglect to do whatever he wants to; he can act properly or improperly, talk or be silent, dress this way or that, go out or stay at home—in any event antipathy's first impulse is to see the negative side, which makes it impossible to see fellow man in his reality. Parents, teachers, catechists and priests—in short, all those who through their profession have an influence on others—should, through self-education and practice, learn to become aware of their antipathies and strive for more disciplined self-control. Antipathy can distort man's relationship with man, lead to wrong action and, thus, render a conscious education impossible.

Antipathy can be directed as well toward religion; not, of course, against God, the invisible, but rather in the form of a block resulting from negative religious experiences with parents, priests, teachers and institutions, which experiences be-

[7] There seem to be three prerequisites for marriage: (1) conformity of the partners in regard to the ultimate questions of life; (2) the same scale of values, that is, the same educational level of mind and heart; (3) the same level of affect. The period of engagement is the time of testing and should clarify these factors. Psychotherapists are well aware of the problems of marriage caused through the neglect of these prerequisites. The many sexual neuroses prove that there is little guidance and help toward love as a healthy part of life.

come a part of religion and tend to obscure a child's view of God. A catechist can cause stirrings not only of affection for God, but also of dislike for Him, since antipathy felt for the teacher is unconsciously transferred to the image of God. Years later, when this particular teacher has long been forgotten, the antipathy might still remain an obstacle to religious behavior. Such fixations can be recognized and eliminated only through the power of positive impressions, for instance, a new dynamic relationship with an educator, or proficient guidance in self-knowledge and self-education. The more serious cases would require professional psychiatric treatment. If such consequences are to be avoided, every religious educator must be willing to take for granted certain situations, such as disciplinary difficulties, for example, rather than create a negative scene that might lead to years of fixation.

While antipathy blinds both eyes, sympathy blinds only one; for, although being a preconception, sympathy reacts positively, and the positive is always closer to truth than the negative. But here, too, no matter what the other does, sympathy always gives him the advantage of a first reaction, seen in a positive light. Sympathy, too, changes the color of things, not to black but to pink, thus distorting reality.

It is certainly true that sympathy can be an element of inspiration in the religious realm—as would be the case in one's enthusiastic admiration for a young priest—but sympathy, when colliding with the reality of religion as it actually is, can indeed turn into a great disappointment if it remains naive and undifferentiated.

An original sympathy and antipathy in the religious sphere would be rooted in an instinctive reaction to the mysterious, to the *tremendum* and *fascinosum*. A man of extremely practical dispositions might react to the religious atmosphere with anger, whereas the other extreme makes spiritual life a compulsion. Yet both cases represent reactive, unreflected attitudes toward religion and its cultural manifestations. Such antipathy or sympathy need not yet be directed toward God Himself, for we must distinguish between the unseen actuality of God and certain, time-conditioned forms of His image and resultant experiences that are merely attempts to approach God. The question, however, as to whether we would react with sympathy or antipathy, should God openly appear to us, can be answered only by alluding to the mysteries of salvation and damnation. The pastor will admit such unforeseeable depths and, in any case, try to avoid pressing too hard in matters of religion.

This much is certainly clear that, in view of the law of sympathy and antipathy, human love must be seen as a living expression of the whole person, and that this psychological level deserves as much consideration and effort for conscious development as the next higher, apparently more spiritual, level that is so one-sidedly emphasized in religious considerations.

4.

Human love is experienced in various forms in the so-called classical forms:[8] parental love, child's love, love of friendship, conjugal love, love of neighbor and love of God. Every form of love contains two basic elements: *intentio unionis,* the desire for union and participation, and *intentio benevolentiae,* the desire for the true good of the other. Both desires will vary in their intensity, and they may manifest themselves together or alternatively. This play and interplay molds the forms of love. An awareness of the diverse conditions of human love gives one an insight into Eros, the psychic capacity of love, and —as a much needed side-effect—allows young people to be set free from the fixation to a single form of love, conjugal love.

In *parental love* both desires are balanced. Parents form a

[8] Cf. Dietrich von Hildebrand, *Metaphysik der Gemeinschaft* (Regensburg, 1955), pp. 51–86.

unity with their offspring in the protecting warmth of which the nestling thrives; he cannot exist by himself, and the parents envelop him with the gifts of their *intentio benevolentiae.* But the more the child grows, becomes independent and detaches himself from the parents, the more should *intentio unionis* diminish. Giving the children their freedom often demands extremely painful renunciation on the part of the parents. Yet, "this willingness to renounce is characteristic of parental love."[9] Parents find it all the more difficult, knowing that children, even as they are breaking away, still require their elders' care. This situation, however, stimulates the *intentio benevolentiae* and directs parental love toward making the child independent and themselves unneeded. They understand that the child must become ready to face life. Once the child has gone on his own, both desires are then restricted to particular situations where help is needed. With advancing age, the possibility of *benevolentiae* lessens, and the possibility of *intentio unionis* reawakens for the parents in the opportunity of spending their evening of life being lovingly cared for by the offspring.

The *child's love,* in its first stage, knows only the *intentio unionis.* The child depends on and is nourished by the parent. The *intentio benevolentiae* is awakened by requesting the child to perform little services for others and giving him a responsibility to help at home. This tends to grow until the child leaves and establishes his own home, remembering his parents in grateful love even from a distance. When aged parents are invited to live in the same house with their offspring, the desire for union and the desire for true good of the other are counterbalanced.

In the *love of friendship,* both partners, so to speak, stand side by side; they face, not each other, but rather the world of values in which they mutually enrich each other. The theme

[9] *Ibid.,* p. 59.

of this form of love is to experience art and the world together, to inspire each other through dialogue. One is to the other, so to speak, the prism through which he sees the world, art and God. Their intent is a limited sharing, not a complete union. The goal is approached together. Such friendship is a gift of God for unmarried people.

When friendship develops into *conjugal love,* the two turn toward each other. Here *intentio unionis* and *intentio bene-volentiae* interpenetrate. The theme of this encounter is no longer *something* outside of this relationship, but the other himself; not something *of* him, but the person himself. Hence the reason why this form of love has the strongest challenge: it awakens the person to open up for the other. Every defense of objectivity is left behind and the I, as it is, confronts the Thou unprotected. This "looking into each other's eyes" ex-presses the inner contact of both persons, which is an incom-parably deeper contact than any possible in the world of matter.[10] In the depth of the person, individuality opens itself up for the other and enters a dialogue. The dialogic structure of the person is actualized.

The result is not only a "special kind of total alertness,"[11] which for many represents the highpoint of their inner devel-opment, but also a characteristic capacity of seeing the other, which here can reach its full development and thus become effective in other areas of life.

Why does a gesture of the beloved's hand fill the lover with delight, as poets have depicted it a thousand times? What does he see? What can he now see that he could not see before? The motion of a hand, for instance, may simply indicate the road to take. The hand—awkward, shackled to the arm, merely part of the organism—is only an indicator of the right direc-

[10] *Ibid.,* p. 51.
[11] *Ibid.,* p. 76.

tion. It is an empty hand, without psychic life. Many entertain this kind of relationship with their body; they only partly occupy it, without ever raising it up from its vegetative level. It has not really become body but has remained a thing. Its task is simply to serve. Hygiene and proper care foster its health, see to it that it functions without disturbance so that it can fulfill its service. But still the body fails to be an expression of the psyche; the psyche is not incarnated in it.

Conjugal love, however, in which *intentio unionis* and *intentio benevolentiae* permeate each other, and in which the one desires to give himself to the other, calls the psyche to fully incarnate itself. The psyche wants to become visible. It takes possession of the body and expresses itself in it, raises it to an *inspired* body and becomes visible in the gesture of one's hand, the expression of one's face, the sound of one's voice. Corporealization makes the body transparent. The more the psyche dwells in the body and incarnates itself—becomes flesh—the more the body becomes transparent for it. The psyche then not only speaks in and through the body, but also expresses and becomes expression. Corporealization and transparency condition each other and fuse into a union.

The other person is called by this—he is reached. He becomes aware, and he sees spirit in flesh. His power of vision is intensified, his eye now open to a new dimension: the presence of the spiritual in the material. He now has become capable for symbols, for he has experienced the presence of the spiritual in the material. Thus human power of love is the impulse for *corporealization, transparency* and *capacity for symbols.*

In the true symbol[12] the spiritual is not merely suggested by the material, as though the spiritual is something hidden beneath the material surface. Rather, the material is put to serv-

---

[12] Cf. Paul Ascher, "Das Symbol," in *Vierteljahresschrift für wissenschaftliche Pädagogik,* 36, I (1960), 25–44.

ice, is transformed, so that it shows the spiritual in a new form of existence, as a union of spirit and matter. Correlated with it is a new capacity of seeing, that is, the capacity for symbols, which presupposes that the person himself is a similar being in his duality of spirit and matter, body and soul—the union of which reaches the heights of corporealization through the power of love. We could say that corporealization makes a person resonant to that which is corporealized. One who has himself become transparent will be able to see the transparent. Conjugal love generally stimulates this use of all psychic powers, so that the capacity for symbols becomes a precious gift of this love.

If this capacity for symbols becomes a conscious state of awareness, the beloved not only becomes transparent, but the lover may also see that a certain flower, or some scenic view, can be the expression of the being of the beloved. Thus a new dimension of the entire world is discovered: its transparency! Hence for him who develops this capacity for symbols, the world, the entire cosmos, becomes transparent: clouds, plants, animals, the elements of fire, water, air and earth—everything is transformed as though in a fairy garden.

This unfolding of human nature is more difficult today because of the one-sided material aspect of civilization with its automatic push-button machines and technical complexity.[13] But what is even worse, many divest themselves of the opportunity of natural development by actualizing Sexus before Eros has had the possibility to unfold. Common decency allows for Sexus to stand back and Eros to unfold, so that it discovers transparency and can enter the world of symbols.

The capacity for symbols is a prerequisite for spiritual life in order to discover Him who is hidden behind creation, but who put His stamp upon its origin with the character of the

---

[13] Cf. Theoderich Kampmann, "Der Film, die Technik und das Zwischenreich," in *Verkündigung und Glaube,* Theodor Filthaut and Josef Andreas Jungmann, eds. (Freiburg, 1958), pp. 294–306.

numinous.[14] Insight into symbols is also necessary in the realm of Revelation, so that Jesus Christ, the Epiphany of God, can be recognized in man. The liturgy needs it to portray the hidden presence of the Kingdom of God. Thus the concern of pastoral care is also to awaken and cultivate this vital "organ," this capacity for symbols, by seeing love life in the context of the basic Christian concept—Incarnation.

Religious education is particularly well disposed to achieve this, since every classic form of love possesses to some degree this power to call for corporealization, transparency and the capacity for symbols. For instance, when a mother lovingly bends over the child, love and protection become expressed in her face. A child, looking expectantly into his parents' eyes, has the innocent face of trust, of unshaken confidence in another, which is the Christian model for the step to faith (Matt. 18:3). The face of a friend enthusiastically expounding a philosophical idea radiates love for truth; hence, truth is witnessed. In any event, Eros is at work, the power that permits a loving relationship with every environment.

One of the laws of the capacity for symbols is of special importance for spiritual life. The spiritual, shining through the material, calls, delights, awakens, inspires, attracts; and man wants to stretch out his hand to it, but when he does, the magic disappears. The rose is no longer transparent when the viewer moves so close that the botanical structure of the leaf can be seen. Distance is an element of vision, and especially of transparent vision. The beloved beckons and promises fulfillment the closer the other comes; but true knowing must keep its distance. The mysterious cannot be touched; it is not to be desired, to be groped for or to be possessed. More exactly, one must not expect to find fusion, for the spiritual world

---

[14] Cf. Romano Guardini, *Religion und Offenbarung* (Würzburg, 1958), I, 21 ff.

is preserved only through distance. "Why does everything beautiful take hold of us, instead of our grasping it?" asks Walter Flex.[15] Obviously, some sadness is always mixed with enthusiasm, like an acid, for preventing spoilage.

It is difficult to see the incarnation of the spirit with its promise of fulfillment and at the same time to be kept at a distance—yet this very experience seems to be important, not only for life as a *person,* but especially for spiritual life. The following levels of this experience are possible: (1) One can desire to become fused with the beloved and suffer the loss of transparency. (2) The disappointment can manifest itself in resignation or even skepticism regarding the reality of true transparency by lowering it to the category of illusion. (3) One can go to the other extreme and emphasize only distance, entering a purely tactical relationship to everything valuable and beautiful, with a proudly reserved attitude of noninvolvement—this is aestheticism. (4) Finally one can aim at the real goal, and through the interplay of closeness and distance learn to find a foothold within the self that makes it possible to open up and be ready for conversation, admiration, reverence, adoration, that is, enter into a true dialogue. No fusion or amalgam is possible between two human beings, but rather a confrontation in the perlucid and tough reality of the difference, yet with all the possibilities of a personal encounter that enables a union much deeper than fusion. This means that in the realm of the person there is no complete fusion—no becoming one thing. I remain I and you remain you. One must be someone, must have found oneself and have experienced the significance of existence in order to be able to have an authentic encounter, that is, to be challenged, called and confronted without permission to fuse, since fusion would mean the loss of the self and hopeless dependency. Instead, the possibilities

[15] Cf. Walter Flex, *Der Wanderer zwischen beiden Welten* (München, 1940).

of seeing, knowing, accepting and conversing open up, which is contact in a much deeper sense of the word: a union of persons, for which married love can then become expression.

The same law of distance rules in the spiritual life. To pour oneself into God with religious enthusiasm and love, like a drop of water into an ocean of bliss, or to be ecstatically lifted out of oneself and to lose oneself, is a wide-spread idea of the Christian goal that unconsciously advocates a non-Christian doctrine of fusion![16] Buddhism, for instance, teaches the relinquishment of the I to the divine Being in which the *individuum* dissolves. But can a psyche be dissolved, once it is awakened to self-consciousness, to self-possession? In other words, when it is living *personally?*

The Christian God is *personal.* He does not want His followers to lose themselves in Him, for if they did, He could no longer converse with them. Such a follower would at best imitate Christ, but not follow Him! The spirit of the liturgical prayers shows us how much God loves confrontation, conversation with grown-up "sons" and "daughters," even though it manifests itself in forms ranging from the most prosaic service to adoring worship. In religion it is even more difficult not to be permitted to melt away but to accept an open confrontation, where God is there and I am here, in a duality that preserves identities and becomes a union of mutual seeing, knowing and accepting. This is the critical point where the right-of-existence before God finds its confirmation. Dialogical encounter is the foundation of partnership with God to which He Himself invites: "I will be his God, and he shall be my son" (Apoc. 21:7).

On the *personal* level human encounter and divine encounter find a parallel; the former is an exercise preparing for the

---

[16] Cf. Walter Schubart, *Religion und Eros* (München, 1941). Here is presented the idea of a religious fusion that cannot be superseded by a personal vision. See also Stöckle, *Gottgesegneter Eros,* pp. 161–169.

latter. In order to enter a real partnership with God, the dialogical way of being must be actuated.

The capacity for symbols is also necessary for the other two classical forms of love, love of neighbor and love of God. In the *love of neighbor,* the *intentio benevolentiae* seems to be clearly predominant: "It hastens to the other, in the fullest sense, but not to be united with him but to enfold him with goodness."[17] It does not expect love in return, nor does it see the other under the aspect of individuality, a fact which runs the risk of reducing him into an object of one's practice of charity and of hurting his, perhaps quite concealed, human dignity. After all, what kind of union could one hope to have with a disreputable human being, almost beyond the possibility of any change? How unlikely that one could be willing to love him in such way that love of neighbor would also include the *intentio unionis?* And, yet, if we care to look more deeply, we can see the hidden, buried, perhaps never acknowledged, core of the *person,* according to which he is called into the Kingdom of God: where "the former things have passed away"; and where there shall be neither "mourning, nor crying, nor pain any more" (Apoc. 21:4); and where this creature shall unfold the self that was given to him and become what he is actually meant to be, in order to participate in the community of God's people! Such an attitude would be the affirmation of his individuality in view of the future. And even more, to the degree that faith is realized, one's capacity increases to see the hidden presence of the future; moreover, in its extreme, it can move saints to embrace the leper. But even a moderately developed faith could stir up at least a presentiment of the hidden presence of the divine call and thus render an authentic relationship possible. To see the other in such manner *in conspectu Dei,* in the sight of God, demands not

---

[17] Cf. Hildebrand, *Metaphysik der Gemeinschaft,* p. 83.

only an effective capacity for symbols in the natural realm but also at least a minimum of the realization of faith.

Considering the love of God from the viewpoint of the two classical elements, we should be able to find in the *intentio unionis* traces of all other forms of love. Just as the renunciation of *intentio unionis* is part of parental love—and parents should not be fearful when the children leave—so the Christian should not be fearful when God departs and is no longer felt as a reality. It could very well be that God's withdrawal produces an effect similar to the interior maturing of the parents when they endure the birth pangs of consciously accepted resignation to their children's departure. By this we mean that the willingness to give up a religious closeness to God, the acceptance of the pain of darkness, turns into a birthpang that chastens one's love for God.

The child's love for his parents should teach us how to face the world with courage. Without staying in direct contact, he will for a long time remain in a secret agreement with his parents, who trust him. Likewise a Christian should have such a secret agreement with God; confident that God trusts him, he dedicates himself to his profession—especially when he is, at times, no longer supported by an intensive, direct relationship with God in his religious life, but must rely on this secret agreement.

Love of friendship, such as we are allowed to have with Christ ("No longer do I call you servants . . . I have called you friends" [John 15:15–16]), is the honor and preference of being chosen. The Christian should make himself worthy of it by cultivating love of friendship. But in such friendship Sexus and Eros must be clearly distinguished, lest a sordid sentimentality enter into it. Practice in the law of distance needed for transparency enables one to become a partner in such a friendship.

Besides these parallels to other forms of love, the *intentio*

unionis toward God can manifest itself directly in a relationship with the divine Persons. Their invisibility, however,
leads us to three reflections concerning the *intentio unionis*:
1. God is to be sought in the realm of the inner world, and
meditation leads the way. 2. The hidden present, shown in
the liturgy, is the most visible point of attraction for *union*.
The life of Jesus lived in the Church throughout the year opens
the dialogue by making present His historical words and
deeds. This is not just the material for a dialogue with God,
but also the practice, nourished by the spiritual experience of
centuries and by the most sublime Christian figures. Liturgical education and a corresponding shaping of the mystery-
celebration could make use of our sadly neglected capacity for
symbols, which, after its first awakening in the forms of
human love-life, often atrophies from lack of practice. Here is
the opportunity for pastoral care to revitalize true conversation with God. 3. The third direction leads us, surprisingly,
to the world. Christ identifies Himself with our fellow man:
"As long as you did it for one of these, the least of my breth-
ren, you did it for me" (Matt. 25:40). Herewith He calls for
the *intentio benevolentiae* in regard to our fellow man, and,
what is more, He refers to Himself as being present in this
other (Matt. 25:35–36). The *intentio benevolentiae* and the
intentio unionis are here joined together, and the invisible can
be loved and cared for in a visible way. Love for God and love
for neighbor are united through Christ.

Why not propose a still more daring idea? Could not all
work, in all areas, as part of the formation of creation, be
directed toward Christ? This would mean, analogically, of
course, and with less intensity, that Christ identifies Himself
with the world of which He is the head. Thus love of God and
love of the world would also form a union, and the specific
age group that performs services for the world could find the
possibility of spiritually penetrating its work and professions

while simultaneously lifting the world of work into the religious realm.[18]

5.

Even a theological reflection on the human capacity of love speaks about a synthesis replacing the duality of religion and the life of love.[19] Opinions about this idea range from reciprocal disturbance to mutual support. We know Nietzsche's statement that Christendom gave Eros poison to drink. While not dying from it, Eros nevertheless suffered a bad conscience. Every misuse of Eros points a finger of accusation or suspicion and tries to banish Eros from religious life. And yet Eros and the life of the spirit are dependent on each other. Whoever separates Eros and religion and sows enmity between them creates a conflict between love for man and love for God. When Eros and religion exclude each other, Eros becomes vulgar and religion frigid. Eros sinks to the level of animal lust, and religion is lifeless. For it is Eros that loosens the ground of the soul, making the mind willing and malleable and cultivating the powers of enthusiasm without which the spiritual life grows weary. When Eros and religion form a union, Eros is ennobled, spiritualized, transfigured, and, in turn, fills religion with vitality. Both have much in common as to their laws of life and should work hand in hand. But they also have a deadly enemy in common—egotism. For both

[18] Cf. Romano Guardini "Theologie der Welt," in *Sorge um den Menschen* (Würzburg, 1962), pp. 71–86: ". . . up to the present, Christian consciousness has recognized positive and negative tasks 'in' the world; but it has not—or, at least, not clearly enough—recognized that the world itself is a task set for it, demanding Christian responsibility" (see p. 85).

[19] Regarding the question of Christianity and sexual life, see Schubart, *Religion und Eros;* Josef Fuchs, *Die Sexualethik des Heiligen Thomas von Aquin* (Köln, 1949); Adolf Eberle, "Geschlechtskraft und Menschenwürde," in *Hochland,* 44 (1952) 391–400; F. X. Arnold, *Woman and Man, their Nature and Mission* (New York, 1963); Stöckle, *Gottgesegneter Eros;* Josef Goldbrunner, "Heiligkeit und Gesundheit," in *Sprechzimmer und Beichtstuhl* (Freiburg, 1965).

thrive on altruistic dedication to others, and both try to attain the same goal: liberation from the I, moving from the part to the whole, that is, from isolation to communion with others. There is a difference, however, between Eros and religion, not in the sense of a rivalry or antithesis, but in the fact that Eros stops halfway and leaves only a premonition of the meaning of final liberation.

But even though Eros cannot bring complete fulfillment, it is nevertheless rooted in religion, since it points back to the time of creation. F. X. Arnold puts it this way: "Sexual pleasure in marriage must be seen as the God-willed creative joy of those who continue and complete the work of the Creator according to his own plan."[20] Eros also points forward to the Kingdom of God at the end of time, since the parables of the heavenly wedding feast suggest that those who wed should understand something of the *eschata*. All this implies that Eros has been created "unto God."

Once the positive religious content of Eros has been established, it is possible, without being derogatory, to accept the meaningful term *Eros thanatos*.[21] "It does not die, but it is always dying." Eros blossoms, unites human beings, but also fades and dies; it blossoms again, only to fade once more; it is a "being of death." Eros is unable to sustain a human relationship over long periods of time unless it is supported by other forces, the forces of loyalty and trust. This means that one who succumbs to Eros must become aware of it and be able to release himself from its grasp. Eros is not the driver of the carriage of the soul, but only the horse that draws it (Plato). Thus it can merely provide access to a person, awaken a person, but the person must be able to rise above it. Eros guides, draws and pushes toward the other, but only when one can see Eros in its true light can it lead to an encounter that is not merely an apersonal, natural event. Identification with Eros

---

[20] Arnold, *Woman and Man,* p. 134.

[21] Cf. Josef Bernhart, *De Profundis* (München, 1952), pp. 129 ff.

unleashes psychic mechanisms that prevent a clear view of the other and that close the psychic realm to *personal* encounter. This is where depth psychology comes in. It provides insight and helps a person to differentiate himself from Eros.

6.

Depth psychology was developed from psychotherapy and is the systematic compilation of and theoretical insight into the anthropological prerequisites for the practice of the cure of souls. Conversely, however, we can say that depth psychology has different fields of application: in medicine as psychotherapy; in pedagogy as guidance; and in pastoral care as anthropological foundation.[22] In dealing with the unconscious, depth psychology broadens the reality of psychic life and thus uncovers a new realm of the reality of creation for systematic investigation.

Unconscious psychic provinces influence conscious life in various ways; one of them is *projection*. Projection is a mechanical process, and its application in depth psychology implies that it is thought of as a psychic mechanism. A picture is projected on a screen by the projector in such way that he who sees it for the first time, or even he who succumbs to its fascination in movies, becomes a victim of illusion and at times finds it difficult to distinguish the reality of the screen from that of the picture projected on it. Primitive man would have to actually see for himself the mechanism of the process and switch the button on and off in order to understand his illusion.

The same sort of projection is at work once Eros has effected a condition of "being in love." The lovers see each other in a brilliant splendor that blinds them to reality. Lover and beloved see each other as they are really intended to be, in a perfection similar to that of creation before the fall. This

[22] Cf. Josef Goldbrunner, *Personale Seelsorge* (Freiburg, 1955), pp. 16 ff.

is the reason why their fascination is a kind of religious experience that at times can open up even the toughest of young men to higher ideals for the sake of his beloved. Then it happens that one of the lovers is disillusioned by some action of the other or by the banality of everyday life—and the magic suddenly vanishes. The other asks himself as if waking up from a dream: "Was I blind? What was I actually seeing? He (or she) is now indeed quite different." This can be a shock, but it offers the possibility of understanding the psychic mechanism of projection.

What the lover had been seeing was real, but like the real in the hallucinations of a high fever. From his own interior, his unconscious, he projected onto the other the image of the ideal partner. It was the power of love concentrated in an unconscious presentation. Depth psychology terms the image projected onto the partner the *Anima* (in the male) and the *Animus* (in the female). Both images are experience-complexes or experience-schemata, "inhabitants" of the unconscious part of the psyche, called archetypes by C. G. Jung in his studies of depth psychology.[23] We are not concerned here with the theory of their origin—whether they are innate like an organ; or formed through the experiences with mother, father, sister, brother, playmates, and so forth; or a combination of both—but only with their effectiveness manifesting itself when we come in contact with someone who makes an unusual impression on us because of something in him that corresponds to the archetype. The Anima (or Animus) then becomes virulent and is projected. The person on whom the image is projected is, as it were, the bearer of a part of the projector's psyche. If the projectee is absent for a period of time, the projector feels that a part of himself has also gone, since projection mechanically causes him to be dependent on the other. Projection occurs like a natural catastrophe, since it is not a

[23] Cf. Josef Goldbrunner, *Individuation* (Notre Dame, 1964).

free event, that is, not the result of a decision, even though it is generally accepted without resistance.

But as long as there is a naive projection, no personal relationship is possible. Man is in the grip of the unconscious, is fixated by a psychic mechanism. Therefore this relationship of "being in love" is pre*personal*. To be overwhelmed by such a projection is equivalent to being enslaved by Eros. To dissolve it leads at the same time to a liberation from Eros and gives access to a *personal* love relationship.

Merely to admit to oneself intellectually the fact that projections can exist is of no help in effectively freeing oneself from them. The evidence of the projected reality so dominates and intensively affects the senses, and consciousness is so convinced by an abundance of pleasurable feelings, that only the experience of the mechanism contrary to projection, namely, its obliteration, can be of help. A disappointing action of the other can suddenly, temporarily or permanently, erase the projection and free the sight for the reality of the other. This is the propitious moment for a differentiation between Eros and its mechanical operation.

If a projection manifests itself again, be it with the same or with another partner, the situation then becomes quite different; there is something in the psyche that refuses to be absorbed by it, keeps its head above water and keeps its distance. It is a premonition of the blindness caused by a complete identification with the projection. "I want no more fiascos, but want to keep my eyes open to reality, to be able to distinguish between the splendor of being in love and seeing the other as he really is." This intention blends into a new projection, first in the form of distrust of self, but gradually becoming "knowledge," gratefully received, so that the "pain" of the earlier disappointment is accepted with a smile and its value recognized. Even though the new projection also occurs mechanically, there is now an authority that can distinguish and responsibly decide in what form a relationship can endure.

Regardless of the impact of a new projection, something in the psyche—existentially realizing the possibility of projection and the intermingling of the Anima and the objectively real—cautiously strives to distinguish the reality of a new vis-à-vis from the projected splendor. In so far as this differentiation is successful, one is now capable of seeing the other as he really is, and the way is open for a true meeting of both: an authentic encounter can take place. Two human beings now truly converse with each other, not united or separated by illusions and prejudices, but entering into a dialogue. The person's *dialogical way of being* is actualized. Seen under the aspect of depth psychology, the experience of projection and its consequent dissolution causes the following changes in the psyche:

The capacity of love becomes a part of consciousness, leading to spiritual permeation and possession. Consciousness becomes broader and is sustained by an inner premonition about the breadth and depth of the soul, about both its light and dark side, for the Anima also incorporates all the dark, soft, receptive, feminine elements of psychic dispositions. The Anima is the "organ" for the feminine aspect of the cosmos (the Animus expresses the masculine aspect). The whole of this psychic province is linked and yoked to consciousness. The masculine-accented conscious of the man is united to the feminine unconscious and vice versa. The man who achieves this kind of integration gives the impression of being "animated"—the reason why C. G. Jung introduced the term *Anima* for this part of the soul. If, however, the Anima is excluded from consciousness, for example, by repression or evasion, a man gives the impression of being "soul-less." In middle age the forfeiture of the Anima causes an increasingly serious loss of vitality, flexibility and humanness."[24] There is

[24] Cf. C. G. Jung, "Über den Archetypus," in *Zentralblatt für Psychotherapie,* IX (1936), 274. The purely psychological use of the concept of *Anima* in Jung's depth psychology is to be clearly differentiated from the metaphysical concept of *Anima.*

ample evidence, therefore, in spite of medieval opinions, that the capacity of love is important not only for sexual life but even more in the *personal* life.[25]

The distinction of the Ego from the Anima makes it possible to confront this capacity of love—to view it objectively. Psychic life becomes differentiated; the budding, naive, undifferentiated experiences develop into a hierarchy. Just as a thunderstorm down in the valley viewed from a mountain top does not lose its violence, so the psyche experiences itself as both mountain and valley. Eros, through the mechanism of projection, causes a thunderstorm in the valley; but simultaneously a directing authority becomes noticeable, standing above and clearly differentiating itself as superior. This is a new height in the experience of the Ego, or it can even be described as a secret counselor confronting the Ego, comparable to the political sense. When a king has conquered and explored a new province, he includes this new part of his kingdom in all his future decisions, since the whole is a living organism. Such far-sightedness manifests political acumen for the common good. Likewise the new hierarchical authority in the psyche represents the ruling center, or its head. This is the *person*. His actualization progresses with the development of the capacity for encounter. He is called upon to develop another side of his structure, his dialogical way of being. At the same time the psychic realm is pierced through all the way into the *personal* realm. Personal encounter becomes possible, even with God. The capacity for encounter renders possible a partnership with God.

Religious education strives to further the capacity for encounter. The formation of youth communities provides the opportunity to create an atmosphere wherein, by protecting and helping, it permits young people to meet one another, in spite of the risk involved. Of course, the *law of encounter* must be analyzed and recognized as a guiding line.

[25] See above, p. 109, fn 19.

Encounter among young people has a beginning, a climax and an end, that is, there is the passing of one by another: an actual encounter. Thus, from the very beginning, the end should be taken into account—the fact of parting again—and this should be possible without damage to either, without reproaches and injuries. Therefore an encounter among young people is fruitful and enjoyable only when self-control is exercised. The fairy tale reflects the wisdom of the law of encounter based on the experiences of generations. It dramatizes, both positively and negatively, the psychic event of encounter.

A person caught up in a projection is like the king's son in a well-known fairy tale. He is on his way to the castle, which lies on the other side of a circle of fire and a deep forest, where the precious stone or the cup of wisdom is awaiting him. The journey through the fire and impenetrable forest is full of dangers and adventures. He has been warned that he must neither talk nor eat during his trip, no matter how alluring the magic figures of the forest; otherwise he will be turned to stone.

Every "youngster with a future" resembles this prince for whom a kingdom is waiting. With his courage to leap over the transforming fire or, in other words, to face the challenge of "being in love," he accepts the adventure of the forest. The forest is the unknown and unpredictable time of the encounter that must be risked. No paths are ever charted; each man must be on the lookout to find his own way; he is on his own and must take the responsibility. Sexually, he must neither "talk" nor "eat"; otherwise he will come to a standstill in his maturing and, like his predecessors met on the way, will turn into stone. Only the angel of penance, touching him, could call him back to life. But if he withstands the temptations of the land of love, and if he respects the law of encounter that allows him the total expression of his desire only in the personally decided, final union of marriage, then he will safely reach the castle and once again find security, home and drink from the cup of wisdom. He has acquired the experience necessary to establish a marriage, a household and home: his "kingdom." During his journey through the forest, where the law of encounter rules—no talking, no eating—sexual realization would not be *personal* expression but only instinct mechanically put into action through a relationship founded on projection. He would become fixated, and would stay behind himself, perhaps even with a burnt-out heart and himself turned into stone, for he had not drunk from the cup of wisdom. Thus the metaphors of the fairy story that dramatically portray the law of encounter give a warning and, at the same time, allow freedom.

The modes of encounter are numerous, ranging from a silent, distant admiration to the temptation of the adventure of love; from a newly felt pain of being alone to the climax of the love of friendship; from a lonely identification with characters in literature, theater and art to a congenial group of friends filled with the spirit of a common striving for maturity. Discipline, self-control and self-honesty make up the price that has to be paid; but its fruit is the capacity for encounter—also encounter with God.

CHAPTER IX

Solidarity and the Need
of Salvation

C HRISTIANITY is realized not only in the intensively unifying encounter between the I and the Thou, between man and God, but also through community. Just as the one-to-one I-Thou relationship is an exercise preparing for the encounter with the divine Thou, so life in community develops dispositions for relationship with God as the Creator of entire humanity and the Savior who died for all. The community of men is witness to God's love of community and, even more, the tasks imposed by life in community reveal features in the image of God that are pertinent to faith. Every belonging to a group brings into the context of living experience the individual's dependence on and solidarity with a group, a nation, with entire humanity in its fate and its history. Questions are now directed at God—pressing, accusing, rebelling, as well as surrendering and accepting questions—all of them decisive stages in the realization of faith. The answers can be found by directing these questions to the Lord of History who raised mere history into a history of salvation. Here again, the categories of religious education and pastoral care must be derived from the symbiosis of man's social dimension and the message of the Almighty Lord of Salvation History, which simultaneously reveal to us that the actualization of man's social dimension becomes effective for the right-of-existence before God through the experience of our need of salvation.

1.

From the aspect of the individual's experience of the significance of his own existence, and the recognition of his right-of-existence before God, the immersion of the individual into a group is humiliating. He is knocked down from his self-made throne of individualism and becomes a number in a row. Yet his rebellious obstinacy does contain a legitimate element, since being reduced to a number is in contradiction to the uniqueness and irreplaceability of the person. This is a degradation! Unless it is possible to actuate a side in the structure of the person that is proper to all men, putting them on a common basis, man cannot mingle among the many without falseness or pseudo humility.

In the same way consciousness reflects the history of our social dimension. The first reaction to life in a group is simply to enjoy the diversity of human beings, the many possibilities of conversation, the abundance of information and stimulation, the mutual help and the sense of belonging. This frequently experienced springtime of the social dimension is followed by a cold spell of often bitter disappointment. The inescapable multitude and its weight become an irritation! It restricts one's freedom of movement. Envy, jealousy, ambition and mediocrity seem to rule. Carping criticism and uncontrolled enthusiasm are tiresome. The confrontation of conservative and progressive tendencies demands constant compromises. How much energy goes into the clearing up of misunderstandings; in fact, at times life seems to be nothing but the juggling of viewpoints. What else can one do but give

up and escape from this "much too many?" The praise of
solitude and the right of the individual are set up against the
humiliating demands of the *massa damnata.*

There is still a third phase, which is not only possible but
even necessary, albeit not reached by everyone. The understanding of the manifold needs of miserable humanity calls
for a willingness to help. Anyone who involves himself in
situations of need and help—which brace up and hold together every form of community—and who overcomes his
resistance and bends, not in pride or condescension, but simply moved by the need of the other, may come to experience
the *solidarity* of all men. In his resonance to others, a new
depth of self-understanding opens up, enabling him to place
himself on the same ground with the others. By this we also
mean ground in the literal sense, the *substratum,* the basis of
all need and the foundation of community. What is it and
how can its existential depth be realized?

2.

The social dimension broadens the I-Thou relationship.
The other is not only orientated toward me, but also has a
background that he brings into this relationship as his title.
Model for this is the change in the I-Thou relationship of husband and wife, occurring as soon as the wife becomes a mother
and now confronts the husband as the mother of his child.
The Thou has changed into a We—she and the child; the
husband becoming the father—he, the mother and the children. The We is always implied. Included also in this We-
relationship are the child, the brother and sister, grandfather
and grandmother, and other relatives. These elements of the
original classical community, the family, create a new situation: the I-We relationship. Not only do the positions of
husband and wife change, but they themselves also change,
broaden, deepen and mature. The challenge of the social
dimension is different from that of the I-Thou relationship.

The next classical form of community is the neighborhood, social or professional sphere in which man lives. External situations condition man for community: the man next door, the school, common profession, his friends. Here again we experience archetypes: the neighbor, the partner, the competitor, the enemy; all are typical. The universal images with their characteristic traits reproduce themselves and, like the Anima, blend into these relationships as archetypes.

The third form of community, the State, also has its archetypes: fellow citizen, soldier, workman, official, statesman, doctor, king, priest.[1] The last three are expected to mediate healing power to the nation, and so they are surrounded by an aura of power.[2] The tyrant, the king of peace, the traitor and the corrupter are experienced as archetypes with the same intensity as are the poor and the rich. Other typical situations are fatherland, homeland, exile, prison, liberation, as well as the parish—a concept so important in pastoral care. All these archetypes appear again as so-called *key concepts* of salvation history and are important in proclamation and catechetics.[3] They touch on realities within man that are filled with the experiences, feelings and emotional values of millenniums. One who knows how to bring them into the consciousness of his listeners speaks, as it were, in a thousand tongues.

All nations are united in the next higher community, which

[1] The possibility of combining priest and king into the priest-king shows clearly that the nation-community contains an element of transcendence.

[2] A democratic and enlightened European will, of course, at first sight reject this. His technically distorted eye sees neither the invisible robe of power in the statesman nor the aura of the priest—until he finds himself in need and the healer is seen in a new light. This can be observed both in emergency situations of an entire nation confidently looking up to its "savior," as well as in individual misfortunes where the priest or the physician is expected to help. Depth psychology speaks here of the projection of the archetypes king, priest, physician.

[3] Cf. Josef Goldbrunner, "Urbilder—Schlüsselbegriffe—Archetypen," in *Katechetische Blätter* (January, 1964), pp. 1–6.

is mankind. When this community is realized, not only does the Frenchman confront the German, the American the Chinese, the Israeli the Arab, but the unchanging differences of nations that reveal God's wealth are likewise grasped at a much deeper level, where all are equal and are simply called human beings. The archetypal basis of mankind is human brother and human sister. In spite of today's awareness of the importance of a united human race, these two archetypes are relatively seldom experienced and only in extraordinary situations. The most universal characteristic of man, to be a human brother or sister, is generally obscured, or buried. Yet its realization is the beginning of a legitimate participation in community, of a "getting into line," since this touches something common to all men regardless of their number. Just thinking about this is not enough; rather, the brotherhood of man ought to be realized in such way that it affects one's existence, that it calls the *person* and actualizes a new side of its structure.

The formulation of the specific tasks imposed upon the human community also point in the same direction. Generation is entrusted to the family; the neighborhood forms the culture; the State ministers to justice, order and welfare; but humanity is concerned with salvation and misery. All men, without exception, are involved in this; and this is an urgent situation, not merely in a negative sense in view of the present political constellations, but also in the positive sense of the pressing obligation to assume more responsibility for the whole of humanity. Suppose that the human race should develop into a political unity, then with instinctive force the important question about its goal would come up; and if it is to be a goal that is more than mere welfare, we must search for the answer in terms of meaning, salvation, damnation. Humanity as community penetrates into the metaphysical situation in its search for possibilities that are beyond those within the world. When this metaphysical situation is constellated through a great common disaster, it awakens a sense of belonging-together, similar to that experienced in a dire emergency by the members of a family, or by the citizens of a state. With a great natural energy, the solidarity of all comes to the fore, along with a deadly indignation toward whatever endangers the real or presumed fortune of all.

But we are still in a stage of development wherein each individual, each one in himself, must realize the metaphysical situation, must be planted deep in his own ground and become a brother and sister in the human community. To consider oneself, with the best of intentions, as brother or sister is certainly a preparation for life in community. The intention "I will be good to all" is the beginning of human kindness. Sentiment and will create a readiness, but it takes a powerful impulse stirred by the situation of need and help in order to push to the depths where one's existence is encountered and implicated. We shall demonstrate this through three situations:

(1) Saving someone's life
(2) Guilt
(3) Responsibility for community

3.

Suppose that a man is drowning. At the risk of his own life, another jumps into the water and saves him. Why? He does not know him, but nevertheless is interested in him. He has no dealings whatsoever with him, and yet without a second thought, almost instinctively, he comes to his rescue. Although the drowning man is not an individual Thou to the rescuer—he's just someone yelling for help—a close relationship, overpowering all inhibitions, comes suddenly to the fore. True, compassion does introduce the inner movement, but compassion alone is not enough to explain the risk of one's own life. A deeper reality breaks open, of which compassion is but a symptom: it is as if new energies emerge out of the depths of the individual, overriding every rational consideration. It is like a universal life-instinct that does not let another simply perish. The unknown stranger has changed into a human brother.

Anyone who has had a like experience knows that this relationship is as realistic as it is real, as primitively human as it is liberating. Similarly, comradeships among soldiers welded together by need and help often last a lifetime because of this very experience of existential depth, even though official citations use other terms. Since genuine existential experiences, such as these, are so rare—perhaps only once in a person's life, or not at all—we can understand why people cling to traditions in spite of the many changes brought about by time. It also explains the tremendous power of genuinely human "material," which, as could be said, one "tastes" when brother and sister of the human race are constellated. It seems that when physical misery is experienced together, all the individual, separating and generally isolating traits melt away and make way for pure human material to come forth—miserable and yet precious. Only then does an individual learn that the other is created to be helped, just as he himself is, and a deep, taken-for-granted, authentic union is gratefully experienced. This is the birth of solidarity.

What we experience on the psychological level as solidarity is, in the *personal* sphere, the person orientated to its origin. This person has not always been, has a beginning, is created, is a creature. The person shares this creatureliness with every other person, so that in this respect all are equal. If a situation psychologically forces an individual into solidarity, a new structural side of the person is simultaneously activated: his creatureliness. It enables the person to become a number without being humiliated, to declare his solidarity with all men, to help the others and suffer with them[4] rather than to exclude

[4] Psychotherapy bases group therapy on the constellation of the "we." If it is well directed, the therapist can effect an existential deepening within the participants by which they, on the one hand, can over-

himself from the common fate. Consequently, he is often set free from the fixation to and the overestimation of his I-Thou love relationship, so that it can find its right place as *one* area rather than *the* area of life. Not only can the We exist alongside the Thou, but it can equally fulfill. This also explains why many problems of love can be solved when the one affected becomes involved in community tasks.[5]

As a further consequence we discover an inner readiness to participate in the community, to integrate and to serve the common interest. This We-relationship, in all degrees of intensity, ranges from a conscious, sober acceptance of certain obligations to a total involvement in community life. Thus creatureliness is realized and summons one to be responsible for everyone.

The friction caused by the interaction of all the individual differences, tendencies and ambitions is less important than another experience that the whole of humanity seems to share: the different answers to the pressing question of the goal of humanity that form the climate of all communities—salvation or damnation. Here the Christian confronts a phalanx of answers, some kind and others hostile, which gradually opens his eyes to another community placed in the midst of humanity—the Church. While embracing humanity, the Church nevertheless points beyond it; she is founded on a definite, concrete answer to the question of salvation, and demands a decision: for it or against it. Universally concerned with the whole of humanity, she penetrates all other forms of commu-

come their neurotic isolation and, on the other hand, realize a healthy relationship to community. Cf. Catherin Küster-Ginsberg's essay, "Die Gruppe als Situation und Mittel zur Begegnung," in *Krisis und Zukunft der Frau,* Wilhelm Bitter, ed. (Stuttgart, 1962), pp. 258–278. Similar group dynamics can be applied in the guidance of youth, in the classroom and in the parish.

[5] This does not mean that the discovery of the *thou* can be replaced by the discovery of the *we*—a practice found quite often in religious education.

nity, changes them, causes divisions and reformations. Thus
the Church is experienced as a special kind of community: concrete yet not tangible, uniting yet isolating, orientating yet
disorientating; while accepting solidarity, she also gives it a
relative meaning.

Belonging to the community of the Church is not self-evi-
dent as is the case of all other classical forms of communities.
The Church presupposes such communities; her experiences
with them are, as it were, her building-material. Thus it is
important from the viewpoint of religious education that a
foundation be laid in the other forms of community, since it
prepares human nature for a foothold in faith within the community of the Church. The experiences gained in these communities alter man, most of all in the human community,
which is orientated to the basis and beginning, and thus by
necessity formulates the question of the end. Whoever has
existentially experienced this human community is ripe for
the great conception of the community of the Church. The life
of faith is in communication with the family, the environment, the State and humanity. All their archetypes are also
key-concepts, key-pictures—or better, patterns—teachings of
faith seen as salvation history.

4.

A second situation leading to an existential deepening of
the realization of humanity as brother and sister is *guilt*. What
is meant here is an actual and grave guilt that affects the community. Here are a few examples: A marriage is dissolved
and the children lose family and home. A physician carelessly
gives a wrong injection, and the mother of many children is
forever in ill health. A priest through his own fault fails to
administer the last sacraments, and the other dies a miserable
death. A drunken driver causes an accident, and the other
suffers an amputated leg. A businessman calumniates a rival
who, as a consequence, loses his position, dies and leaves his

family behind without financial support. A religion teacher deals unjustly with a child in the classroom; the child reacts traumatically and ceases to attend Mass on Sunday. A pastor's misuse of the church collection becomes public, and people lose their confidence in giving to the church.

Common to all these examples is the effect that a culpable action has on innocent people: it never, or hardly ever, can be remedied and is a constant burden for the culprit. Such guilt cannot be wiped off with a quick confession, as can dust from furniture. Guilt, when rightly endured, passes, just as Dante depicted in his *Divine Comedy,* through three stages: "Descent into the hell of pain," a "transformation" and a "resurrection."

a) *Descent into the hell of pain.* Guilt isolates, and it separates one from other people, even if it is not publicly known. It shuts one up in a prison, where the guilt constantly watches over the I. The I is, so to speak, chained to the guilt; or even worse, guilt eats its way like an ulcer into the I, becoming one with the I: "I am evil, I myself am guilty." Guilt is not some part of the I, but the I itself is guilty. The I is weakened and changed, as if suffering from a bad climate that alternately scorches and freezes; it lives in a house where all the furniture is falling apart. Grave guilt dissolves security, even though its effects often may be experienced only much later—and in such cases the effects are all the more inescapable.

In such a situation the I is forced to take a stand. Which one of the three typical possibilities it will choose depends certainly on its stamina, mental aptitude and entire life history. But in the final analysis every decision is impenetrable and unpredictable. Some escape with great violence in self-destroying suicide wherein the courage to die amounts to a fear to live; others slip into a resignation consisting of a mixture of defiance, sullenness, terror and accusations against the fate that has driven them into this guilt. The rest, however, confront the situation without running away; they overcome defiance, pride and euphemistic self-evaluation and accept their guilt. With a peculiar passivity they allow the guilt-feeling to be worked out. They accept the "hell of pain" and enter the second stage.

b) *Transformation.* A change is now taking place, which, if it could be expressed, would be a kind of dialogue with the self: "To be guilty means to be miserable and helpless; at basis this is probably what we all are, miserable beings; the only thing left for us is to be kind. We all are so much in need of kindness." Often, such silent kindness is first directed toward animals, as though experiencing a kind of self-humiliation. But then it is extended to all creatures including men. The depth of misery awakens a creaturely sense of union that no longer questions but simply knows: "That's the way it is." Virgil expressed this with the words *Sunt lacrimae rerum* ("Things have tears"), and Hölderlin says "I love you earth because you grieve with me." The bond of creaturely affection is not sweet but bitter. It is connected with need and help, with suffering and serenity. The ground of existence is sad. The experience is not comfortable, pleasant or sentimental.

c) *Resurrection.* The third stage is a new orientation to life, which has the effect of a "resurrection." A man in this phase is willing to serve the community: with no personal ambition, he joins others; he lives in communication with the many, which is at a depth where individualists no longer irritate one another. He is on the plane where human brothers and sisters meet one another, and every day he feels the others' misery as well as the need in his own inner self. His solidarity is rooted in his own being. He is no longer set in his ways but seems to be understanding and calm. He can listen and wait without impatience and tension. This at times may even seem to be weakness; and, in fact, he is weaker when it comes to superficial matters, into which he no longer puts any energy. His strength is rather concentrated in depth, beneath the surface, in the ground where the roots and beginnings are contained. This is his point of departure for work in communities. He represents the basis of community life, creates a current that draws others into its wake. While on the one hand they feel this as a burden, on the other they find that many difficulties of life in society simply melt away as they assume a relative character in view of the supporting reality of a brother-sister humanity and the reality of the neediness of all.

When a man enters the life of the community, the effects of the "resurrection" take on greater proportions. His mute, animal-like attitude of silence in the face of guilt—for he is incapable of questioning or of begging for help,[6] the "unlamented creature"[7] that he is—broadens out into the prospect of helping whenever he is touched by the collective need of members of the human race. Symptomatic treatment, that is, giving specific kinds of help, such as methods of hygiene to certain groups or training underdeveloped nations in economic self-help, is not enough. This merely treats the symptoms of the great need that runs like an undercurrent through everything. Individual symptoms are not the actual need, for the being-ground itself is in need. Entire humanity, its total being, is in need and presses us to articulate the question of the why and wherefore of the beginning, of the future, of change. This question is all the more urgent and far-reaching whenever the individual need is seen more and more as a part of the collective need. The individual can be helped only in so far as the whole community experiences a change. Thoughts and questions such as these emerge spontaneously and with compelling force, and, even more, being itself has become a question.

Whenever existence is questioned, the answer cannot be based merely on economics, such as a new system of economic aid; nor can it be founded on psychology, that is, alluding to

---

[6] Romans 8:22: "For we know that all creation groans and travails in pain until now."

[7] Cf. Josef Bernhart, *Die unbeweinte Kreatur* (München, 1961).

the correction of hereditary and environmental influences; nor can depth psychology find the answer in self-discovery through psychotherapy, since the self, too, participates in the misfortune. The helpful answer cannot take into account merely the symptoms, for it must be able to heal the source itself. The salvation of the whole is at stake. Question and answer therefore lie in the religious realm. The state of consciousness is determined by the question of damnation and the search for salvation. Thus the experience of guilt existentially constellates the question of religion; the universal *need of salvation* is experienced. This would be the prerequisite for the Christian answer of salvation. The need of salvation must be experienced and recognized in the foreground of Revelation so that man in his very being confronts God in a primordial situation, that of need and help. This allows a fundamental religious relationship, that between creature and Creator. It provides man, the creature, with a correction of the error of measurement in his interpretation of the right-of-existence before God, since he is in need of salvation. Man, capable of, and called to, partnership, confronts the Creator as supplicant.

The need of salvation sides with the right-of-existence and partnership. These three are the fruits of existential experience accompanying *personal* actualization. The corresponding dimensions of the structure of the person are: significance of individual existence; dialogical mode of being; and creatureliness. Creatureliness means to be created, to have a beginning and to share this with all men; to stand together with them on the same bitter ground and, hence, also be able to accept. Creatureliness is the existential basis of the social dimension. Its actualization through the experience of guilt also enables man to truly participate in communities.

Thus when the experience of guilt is explained and brought more clearly into consciousness (man so much needs an interpretation of his own experience of the "descent into the hell of pain," of "transformation" and "resurrection"—and this is so

obviously the core of pastoral care), the result is the actualization of another structural side of the person, making possible
the I-We relationship. At the same time the foundation of religious relationship is laid through the experience of the need
of salvation. If this need of salvation is accepted in faith,
which is the theme of our next chapter, the question finds its
answer. In other words, the readiness of one's whole being
makes possible the acceptance of the message of salvation with
one's whole being: the message is incarnated. Man in need of
salvation surrenders to the salvation brought by the messenger
and Son of the Creator, and allows himself to be saved. The
doctrine of salvation can be realized.

Specific to this newly won solidarity is the insight that in
the life of faith one confronts God the Savior not only as an
individual but also as a member of the community. The need
of salvation is understood in the sense of solidarity, and salvation and redemption are awaited in solidarity. Corresponding to this is the "collective thinking" of the Old Testament
and the doctrine of salvation.[8] Once the concept of solidarity
is present in consciousness, the individualistic interpretation
of salvation broadens into, and is realized as, the salvation
of the community of humanity.

Only if such experience leads to an acceptance of the message of salvation, and especially here of the doctrine of the
sacramental forgiveness of sin, will guilty man be endowed
with the full "resurrection." He who after his descent into the
"hell of pain"; where he has experienced an existential deepening through "transformation"—and after his emergence into
the solidarity of service to men receives forgiveness of sins—
has made an important step forward in his realization of faith.
The need of salvation and the salvific message itself join
together as though an incarnation.

[8] Cf. J. de Fraine, *Adam and the Family of Man* (Staten Island, 1963).
In the concept of "the corporate personality" the concrete individual
stands for the group and the group for the individual.

5.

Taking responsibility in the community is a third way to deepen the social dimension into a collective experience of creatureliness and of the need of salvation. We shall deal first with the experience of *responsibility,* and later introduce three aids to its performance.

The mother of a large family, a director of a plant, a physician in his various roles as private practitioner or member of a hospital staff, an organizer of a convention, the mayor of a city, ruler of a country, pastor of a parish, bishop of a diocese —all these carry community responsibility in this special sense. They bear a burden: they have taken over a task in the service of others in different forms of communities. The experience connected with this responsibility passes through various stages.

Prevailing at first is joy in one's own fulfillment. One can care for others, is available for others, is needed. It is a satisfaction to have been chosen and to have the confidence of others. The new task gives an opportunity to prove oneself and to develop one's capacities. One can realize plans and mold life. One is put at the head of the line to carry out this purpose: one stands higher, sees more. This, however, already creates, by necessity, distance from the others. The "honeymoon" of the office held does not last long, for soon there is an awakening to the reality that now everything one says will have unpredictable public repercussions, and that one's words weigh more than ever before. It is necessary to think of all the consequences beforehand. Many things that previously were merely private matters are now in the public eye. A change in one's attitude, even in one's nature, is the result. Thus, a man who will keep openminded in such a situation and voice his experience without pride or fear would probably say something like this: "I must be available for all, always for others; they come to me with all their worries and at every hour. I feel like a rubber band being pulled at both ends, becoming thinner and thinner in the middle. There is hardly any private life left. In this tensile test it is as if something might die in me, as if my Ego might gradually be extinguished." When, without pride, a person allows this to transpire within himself —expressing his will to concentrate on selfless service, without self-pity or sentimentality, without moaning and groaning, that is, simply dedicating himself and serving, opening himself to the needs and necessities of others—then he begins to feel at the thinnest part, in the slow extinguishing of the Ego, a kind of emptiness followed by a painful fulfillment, as

though a sword has pierced his heart. At this thinnest point he can be penetrated by something that comes from outside, from "above." He has the experience of the cross, not the Christian cross, but the mythological. The dimension of the width into which he is stretched with arms widespread is crossed at its thinnest and most painful point by the dimension of above and below: the dimension of the cosmos is transversed by the dimension of heaven.[9]

At the point of crossing is the opening for another world; here man is permeable to what comes from there, from beyond the threshold of death—just as it is expressed by the presentiments of many pre-Christian religions. He who gives himself selflessly and serves does not know what happens to him; he is, so to speak, in a cocoon spun by time.[10] When the com-

[9] Cf. Hugo Rahner, *Greek Myths and Christian Mystery* (New York, 1963). Odysseus, the traveler in general, on his road as man, is tied to "the giant mast, crossed at right angles by the yard," but his ears are wide open for the sounds of another world. He is the image of the mythical experience of the cross of man (see p. 372 ff); cf. also Hugo Rahner, *Symbole der Kirche* (Salzburg, 1964), pp. 260 ff.

[10] Cf. Leopold Ziegler, *Überlieferung* (München, 1949), especially the chapter titled "Signatura crucis," pp. 501–531.

munity faces a crisis, everyone depends on him and his life-generating decision, since he is the one responsible, in contact with higher powers. But he does nothing, he is indeed in a cocoon: he is crucified at the point where world and heaven, cosmos and Theos, intersect, and he allows himself to be consumed by his responsibility. Then a sudden inspiration restores his capacity for decision; he tears open the cocoon of his inaction and takes the right step to help the community. He mediates healing powers from beyond: to his family, his tribe, his people, his nation. He has saved his people from great danger; and once the danger is overcome and the victory gained, a feast is held. Like all who mediate such power he is now enveloped in a religious aura. It is customary among primitive peoples that a feast take place whenever a god appears, whether in person or in the form of his healing powers mediated by a human being. Life in community not only sheds the "tears" of its need of salvation, but also has joyful festivities whenever, in a situation of need, the helping relationship with the "above" has been realized.

But only he who holds the responsibility for the situation realizes the price that has to be paid—the experience of the cross. It is through this experience that he becomes a "knower," a victim and one of the "elect." He knows that a price must be paid for salvation from evil. It is a presentiment based on the experience of the cross: that salvation is effected through powers coming from beyond the threshold—a threshold to be crossed only through sacrificial death. The pierced heart at the intersection of the horizontal and the vertical dimensions is, in the language of myth, the doorway for the powers of destiny. This is the language both of folklore and of Sacred Scripture: "Thy own soul a sword shall pierce" (Luke 2:35). Such human experience is an exemplar event filled with all presentiments of the world in advent.

What happened on Calvary is the fulfillment of all presentiments, not only as psychic event but also including all external reality. Not only does it repeat the myth of the psychic event of the "descent into hell," the "transformation" and "resurrection," but also the unique historical fact of an actual descent into the source of damnation in order to solve and heal all guilt at its very root. Thus the exemplars of the spiritual event and the message of salvation are interconnected, the same as presentiment and fulfillment, as question and answer. In view of pastoral theology this means that presentiment and question originate in the exemplar-event, and must be interpreted in this sense so that the answer and fulfillment of Revelation can be realized and incarnated.

In so far as the pastor, in serving his parish, undergoes this mythological experience of the cross, he will learn for himself how important and necessary it is to have an understanding of creatureliness in order to accept the need of salvation. His resonance to those entrusted to him, who are on their way to such depth of experience, will help guide them. But, like a sensitive seismograph, he should be aware when pride creeps in and spoils everything, since haughty responsibility leads only to isolation and, like a suit of armor, hinders existential growth. He will, therefore, see the need of being available for service to the public and will also try to inspire others to work with him. To bear responsibility for the community is an important opportunity for the realization of faith.

6.

The difficulties involved in the life of responsibility demand the help of certain allies. Such allies are power, time and diplomacy.

One who has accepted responsibility for others simultaneously is endowed with a certain *power:* father and mother over the children, teachers over the pupils, organizers over groups, the foreman over his workers, the pastor over his flock. All are granted power as a help in the performance of their tasks.

The experience of the possession of power also has a history. One speaks generally about the burden and forgets that it is basically a pleasure to possess power. Power means an increase of one's own possibilities. Whoever has had the opportunity to develop the sense of power knows that, at all times, power has fascinated and will fascinate man. One can play with it and create new possibilities. To be powerful intensifies the sense of life. This is experienced in many little things, particularly when others serve, that is, fulfill one's will, and seem eager to do all kinds of favors. Power can take on many forms: power in education, political power, disciplinary power.[11] Such power goes along with a responsible office in the community. It is necessary to make it one's ally in order to be able to take a stand and make decisions. This, too, may lead to an opening of man's metaphysical situation. A few examples may illustrate the point.

A decision must be made as to hiring an applicant. The consequences of this decision, be they rejection or acceptance, deeply affect the life of another; they change his life and the life of his family. Momentarily the life of others depends on one's decision—power is felt.

A court has reached the point where judgment is to be pronounced. All stand up awaiting the moment that will relieve the tension. Nobody knows yet whether it will be acquittal or punishment. The whole weight of destiny lies upon such a moment. How is this experienced by the judge?

Power over life and death is even more clearly manifested in the strategic perspective in a war which, very much simplified and yet demoniacally exaggerated, goes about like this: "The fate of the individual disappears from one's view, yet these individuals are present to one's spirit and, added together, create an atmosphere that causes terrific pressure."[12] It

[11] Cf. Romano Guardini, *Die Macht* (Würzburg, 1951), especially the chapter titled "Das Wesen der Macht" (English translation, *Power and Responsibility*).

[12] Cf. Ernst Jünger, *Strahlungen* (Tübingen, 1949), p. 260.

is a quality of power, both fascinating and depressing, to be able to play with life, to be able to kill life. Power is the force over life and death.

Prideful power leads to pseudo self-knowledge, since it flatteringly allows one to identify with it. The proud possessor of power considers the capabilities that power has only loaned to him as his own inherent talents. But the feeling of being a kind of higher human being leads to isolation from community and blocks the metaphysical situation.

He, however, who in selflessness and sincerity wears power like a robe or vestment that is merely loaned to him, that can and must be taken off, and who, in spite of his joy and pleasure in the royal robes, repeatedly differentiates himself from them—such a humble man of power, when he finds himself in a situation where he must make a decision supported by the fullness of his power, a moment when all look up to him full of expectation and fear and he feels this power tingling in his hands, may well experience himself as the medium for something that comes from the other side, from a supernatural sphere, and knows that life and death depend on him. In spite of his power, there arises a strong sense of unworthiness. The wielding of power with the controls in his own hand; the look of dependence or of surrender in the other's fearful eyes, the recognition of the limitation of all human life—these can awaken a sympathy for all creation and afford a sense of solidarity. For a moment the metaphysical situation opens up, and creatureliness as the basis of the sense of life enters consciousness. The reality of existence tastes like dry bread; the *personal* sphere is open.

Power seems to have a peculiar fascination for man, and he is easily tempted to identify with it, to abuse it, and thus to distort the distinction between creature and omnipotent Creator. To sense the instability of the heart in a crucial moment, in responsible positions and situations of decisions, in the experience of power over life and death, seems to be an oppor-

tunity for the person to become either open or definitely closed
to the need of salvation. What a challenge, and what a danger!
The experience of power can open a good part of the foreground of human nature for the Christian message, but it also
can close it up by yielding to the temptation of self-exaltation.

The pastor, too, no matter how religious, pious, or even
Christian, be his words and intentions, can succumb to the
hold that power has over him—a fact proving that in so far as
one yields to pride this process takes place only partly in the
conscious and, likewise, only partly in the unconscious through
activation of power-related archetypes. But power can be effectively dealt with only on a superior sphere, which one could
call the "superconscious," or the *personal*. There the power of
free decision can be gained or lost. When, for instance, in spite
of his conscious adherence to Christian verbalizations, a pastor
becomes closed to the concept of creatureliness, the visible
symptom will be an overemphasis of his authority and power
over his parish, a compensation for his loss of solidarity. Then
the preaching of God's Word is no longer an entreaty or invitation, since the priest is not the medium of the Word but
rather a representative of overweening authority.

Time is the second ally of anyone who bears responsibility.
One may, for instance, hesitate in making a decision, postpone
it, for time will help to clarify this and to change that. Time
heals, lets things be forgotten, gnaws at the position of the
opponent, gives rise to developmental changes. He who has
a responsible position can use his power to postpone a decision by means of his authority; he makes time his ally.

The man with authority, however, is tempted to misuse the
element of time: he can keep people standing around, since
they depend on him anyway, and can leave them hopelessly
stranded until they no longer resist. He can try to play the
part of Providence and enjoy his own power and leadership.
This is a usurpation of time.

The right use of time, however, can lead to an experience of depth. Suppose, for instance, that the one in charge has to postpone a decision, since those entrusted to him are not yet mature enough for it, and since he does not want to cut off positive possibilities at the very start, but rather give time for group-forces in the background to form themselves more distinctly and come to the fore. All of a sudden things change; time blocks the decision and the development takes an unforeseen course. Time cannot be stopped, it flows toward an unknown goal; the future is unpredictable. Instead of being an ally of time, he suddenly finds himself its prisoner. The limitation of his own being leaps into his awareness and shakes his whole nature.

What is the root of this limitation? In view of the great possibilities of power, of control, of the importance of his position, of the successes he has had, failure suddenly makes time seem to be something ambivalent, something undermining life, discomposing and dissolving. Transitoriness is seen as something that should not be. It seeps into the ground of life, as would an illness. The ground of life itself is sick. Propitious time shows its other face—time not joined to eternity and thus weakened by the void; its vitality contains a deadly germ; its density of being fades into a phantom. The higher the position of authority the deeper is the experience of such abandonment. Profoundly affected and moved, one questions the possibilities of redemption and salvation. The religious question lies hidden in the ground of the experience of responsibility for the community and rises up spontaneously, as if existence itself is beginning to ask "Is there any way out of this misery?" Time is a chain that must be broken.

The third ally is *diplomacy*. In some instances a leader chooses his words in such a way that he cannot be pinned down by either side. His reservations always give him room to swing the other way. When the majority consents to a change, he is all for it; otherwise, he will be for the status quo. In such instances, diplomacy is merely used to stay on top, to keep the powerful position. It is egocentricity shut away from the situation of responsibility for community; it is noninvolvement with solidarity. But diplomacy is nevertheless a necessary ally of every position of leadership. Human beings differ in so many ways; something easy for one may be too hard for the other. Something can be understood by one, whereas the other is not yet ready for it. Shall the one be allowed to do what is forbidden to the other? Can an answer be formulated in two different ways? Situations such as these are necessarily met by anyone who is in charge of men. The doctor, at times, must conceal from a patient the gravity of his illness; the pastor, at times, must talk with regard to this and that, lest he become extremely formal. Diplomacy does not interfere with responsibility, yet the attitudes toward it may vary.

Some may use diplomacy with scarcely any reflection at all. They think it is merely something that everyone uses in order to reach a goal most expeditiously. They may even have lost their sense of truthfulness. For others, however, diplomacy is a burden. They cannot become reconciled to the fact that they should not tell the truth they know; that they cannot lead as they know they should; that, while the absolute cannot be weakened in its claim, it nevertheless has to become relative in practical life. Only with diplomacy as his ally is one able to serve the common good. This attitude toward diplomacy, so painfully felt, is not the result of a youthful idealism that unconditionally rejects every compromise but is a profound realization of a defect at the very basis of a human community. The resultant suffering, when not repressed; urges toward the ever present question of the need of change, of a solution or even of the need of salvation. Humanity's need of salvation is an existential experience of many who, in their service to the community, are confronted with the problem of diplomacy. The higher one's position, or one's view and power, the more one understands the need of the salvation of humanity. This limitation of power of decision that shakes one's entire being —where are its roots? If the answer lies in the relationship of creature to Creator, the experience of community prepares the soil for the religious question.

CHAPTER X

Conversion and Faith

THE DEVELOPMENTAL step into the realization of the I-Thou-We relationship prepares the *personal* sphere for the encounter between man and God, since by actualizing the person it establishes prerequisites for the encounter with God. As we have seen, every step actualizes a side of the structure of the person. The realm of individuality activates the significance of one's own existence; the realm of love- and sex-life activates the dialogical mode of being; the life in community activates creatureliness. The significance of one's own existence, the dialogical mode of being and creatureliness, are structural sides of the person. Every step has led to an existential deepening significant for the life of faith: right-of-existence before God; partnership with God; need of salvation. It is obvious that the three steps intertwine and no one of them can be perfectly realized. The degree of their realization is the basis of the *personal* sphere, and thus basic for the fourth step, the fourth great task of life, equally as important as the discovery of the I, the Thou and the We: the discovery of God.

The numinous character of the world compels every human being to articulate the question of religion. Whether the answer be positive or negative, life forces him to this confronta-

142

tion. The Christian, however, does not confront merely a numen, but God Himself, God as Person. There can be no real basis for faith without *personal* encounter, since faith is the "salvific encounter between God and man."[1] Thus we are led to these two questions: 1. How does Christ's Person affect the person of man? 2. How can pastoral care aid this encounter?

1.

Man reacts not merely to the other's body, intellect, manifestations of his will and emotions, but also to his *person*. Person is resonant to person like two violin strings vibrating at the same pitch. Thus the mysterious core of man, his *person,* is not grasped by his intellect but only by his person. Consequently one can in fact ask the question: "How does one grasp a person?"[2] It seems that the structural sides of a person should be actualized so that one who has developed his authenticity, his capacity for encounter and his solidarity, evaluates the other in the same way and thus can "grasp" him. When a human person is in resonance with another human person in this manner, it means also that this human person is in resonance with the divine Person. Then man, in his individuality, who lives the truth of himself and who, in the significance of his own existence, has become one with himself, and thus dares in the realization of his right-of-existence to face up to God—this man would encounter the individuality of Christ, the Son of God, who not only is one with His truth and possesses it, but who Himself is truth; who not only rests within Himself in the significance of His existence, but who is the purpose and meaning of all created existence. God

[1] Cf. Max Seckler, *Handbuch theologischer Grundbegriffe* (München, 1963), I, 539. The personal encounter between God and man as a faith-instilling act comes more and more into the foreground. The personal element prevails with no opposition between the "thou-faith" and the traditional "content-faith"; see also Josef Pieper, *Belief and Faith* (New York, 1963).

[2] Pieper, *Belief and Faith.*

Himself, the Son of the Creator of all being, stands before man who insists on his right-of-existence. How will man react to such an encounter? Will he be excited, demanding, frightened, fearful, insecure? Or, in wonderment, will he grasp a deeper meaning and recognition and be encouraged "through a mysterious empathy" to take over his own "uniqueness?"[3]

The second structural side of the human person, its dialogical mode of being, is in the same way confronted with the divine Person of Christ who springs from the eternal dialogue of the three divine Persons and who, with His capacity of encounter for all, can be, and desires to be, the partner—for His love is *Agape.* The third structural side of the person, creatureliness, encounters the uncreated, eternal Person; and nature's need of salvation stands before Him, who, in solidarity with all men, brings salvation, and who descended to the ground of all being in order to heal it. How will such encounter affect the human person?

If it should take place openly, is it conceivable that even then man's freedom would not be overwhelmed and rendered ineffective? One would imagine that surprise could loosen all inhibitions, and that by free decision the words of the elders of the Apocalypse could be voiced: You are "worthy to receive power and divinity and wisdom and strength and honor and glory and blessing" (Apoc. 5:12). It is thus conceivable that from the divine partner flows the confirmation of the human, individual being who has not yet grasped himself to this extent, and that this happiness creates a surrender whereby the person bursts into bloom, making Kierkegaard's words ring true: "The measure for the self always is that in the face of which it is a self."[4]

---

[3] Cf. Karl Rahner, "Der Erzieher," in *Mission and Grace* (London, 1963).

[4] Cf. Sören Kierkegaard, *The Sickness unto Death* (New York, 1941), p. 210. Man acquires his consciousness of the self in distinct gradations: ". . . a herdsman who (if this were possible) is a self only in the

Such fulfillment of all personal capacities would actualize the fourth side of the structure of the person, the *capacitas Dei*. The human person is able to come in contact with the Person of God, to grasp the divine Person in the sense of a knowing, confirming, accepting answer of faith. The person is *capax Dei*—the greatest thing that can be said of the human person. In the personal contact with the divine Person, man will actually transcend, which is the open or secret longing of mankind of all times. Transcendence is the religious fruit of personal encounter with Christ. Person will be called by its authentic name,[5] will be known, affirmed, accepted, confirmed and thus called to fully unfold itself. Such complete being-oneself with its responding attitude is the highest actualization of the person. The human person is called to its full realization in the face of God. The person awakens to its full "name."[6]

If the open encounter with the divine Person does not exclude the freedom of the human person, then it must be possible in this situation to say *no* and to become closed. Here we will not analyze this terrible possibility, with all its consequences, but merely cast a glance at the impenetrable mystery of the decision of one person in the face of another. Even when everything apparent has been evaluated, the final decision is free and unpredictable; it is a creative beginning of a new chain of cause and effect for which one can and must be responsible. This is possible also in regard to God, but here the decision is connected with salvation and condemnation. It is an impenetrable mystery that a human person in this interaction of grace,

sight of cows is a very low self, and so also is a ruler who is a self in the sight of slaves—for in both cases the scale or measure is lacking. . . . But what an infinite accent falls upon the self by getting God as a measure."

[5] Cf. also Romano Guardini, *Welt und Person* (Würzburg, 1962), p. 165: ". . . man is man to the extent that he realizes and accepts obediently the thou-relationship to God."

[6] Ernst Michel uses the term "Namentlichkeit" in *Rettung und Erneuerung personalen Lebens* (Frankfurt, 1951), p. 102.

which is "God's self-mediation,"[7] and his capacity for free decision can close himself to God.

There is another, more important, consequence for pastoral care. If person is resonant to person, then in the proclamation, which speaks about Jesus, something of His Person should be experienced by the listener. This mode of proclaiming the message of Jesus would be just as far removed from subjective sentimentality as from the objective rationality of dogmatic derivatives. No intention of either will or reason can enable one to speak about a person in such way that this resonance is awakened and takes on life. Nor can it be caused by psychological inferences regarding the unique personality of Jesus, but only through an account of deeds and words conjoined with witness. Then speaking about Jesus takes on a characteristic power that cannot be fabricated—the fruit of a personal relationship between the messenger and Christ. What a challenge to the preacher and teacher of Christian doctrine!

The divine Person, however, does not meet us openly, but behind a screen. Thus there can be only a partial and approximate fulfillment of the possibilities of the open encounter. Scripture tells us about the life of Jesus; we believe that He in the "fullness of life" "sits at the right hand of God," and that He, through the mysterious action of the Holy Spirit, *personally* calls each one of us, everywhere, though in a special way through the living manifestations of the Church, that is, through proclamation and liturgy. But He himself is concealed, invisible, accessible only through the mediation of Scripture, the mysteries of the liturgy and other human persons.[8] These conditions make it more difficult to grasp His person. It

[7] Cf. Karl Rahner, "Gnade," in *Lexikon für Theologie und Kirche* (Freiburg, 1960), 4, sec. 1013.

[8] It is clear that Christ Himself works through all these acts. Yet it may also be mentioned that beyond this there are ways that escape the grasp of pastoral theology.

would surely be impossible without the promised help of His calling power (the *pneuma*). Thus learning to know Jesus all the way to the point of encounter implies a preparation in which pastoral care and religious education play a decisive role.

As *Logos,* Christ is orientated to consciousness; the proclamation, interpretation and witness of His teachings address the conscious. But Christ as the bearer of the *numinous* is directed to the natural religious disposition (more precisely called the religious archetypes of the unconscious), and proclamation must work out the discernment of the Christian idea, recognizing both its conformity with and difference from the religious disposition and making adjustments for the difference. The Church year, confronting us with the life of Christ, gives us the opportunity for this discernment. Thirdly, the divine *Person,* the *personal* call of Christ, is present both in Christ the Logos and Christ the bearer of the numinous, calling forth the person and awakening its resonance.

The human person is called to respond, to decide for Christ; and even when this decision must be renewed in the face of challenging crises or because the change into another age group leads to a deeper understanding of Christ, the response is never directed merely to the teachings or to the numinous, but also becomes more and more a response to the Person of Christ. To face this Person; to contact Christ Himself and not alone His teaching; to not merely sense the numinous, but also see Him (in spite of His concealment)—is the encounter between person and Person, is actual transcendence by which the divine Person is touched. Faith thrives on these fleeting moments of grace and becomes strengthened for the periods of distance. Even a single moment of transcendence already indicates the direction that the human person should take to find its way out of isolation and into union with the divine ground of being.

This means that in order to grasp the divine Person, the

human person must apply the same conditions necessary to understand another human person. The aforementioned four steps of *personal* actualization are prerequisites for transcendence.

2.

Pastoral care furthers the faith-building encounter with God through its proclamation of Christ. Christ as Logos is orientated to the conscious, but as bearer of the numinous quality He is related to the natural religious powers, which are nourished by the archetypal dispositions of the unconscious. Both relationships must be skillfully worked out not only in view of a correct interpretation of Revelation, but also in view of human nature so that anthropology and theology have their proper place.

a) The first task is to proclaim Christ in accordance with our situation in salvation-history, the between-time. Christ shows us concretely the four elements of this between-time. The *future dimension* points to Him as the returning Christ. The *concealed reality* of Christ as the Lord of History, *present* in His Word and, above all, in liturgy, makes history transparent. The *personal* call of His message not only constellates our *burden of the past* but also shows us the possibility of gradually overcoming the weakness of our person. Through His way of the cross, Christ engenders confidence in the meaningfulness of *pain* in general and shows us pain clearly as a transition: through death to new life, through pain to resurrection. Through such proclamation the I with its conscious powers directs itself toward Christ as Logos and takes an intellectual stand in accordance with the spiritual context of the individual.

b) Such a decision is not made merely on the intellectual level, but generally made below the threshold, and is unconsciously influenced.[9] This makes us aware of the second task of proclamation that must be performed with equal skill, since a proclamation based on reason does not yet guarantee an encounter with Christ in which He is truly seen. In other words, proclamation shows Christ not only as the crystal-clear Logos, but simultaneously as the bearer of the sacred, of the religious. Something mysterious is attached to His figure, something that is both dangerous and attractive, stimulating the unconscious organs for the numinous. These organs take possession of the figure of Christ, and the decisive question arises whether He is commensurate with them. It could happen that they block the sight of Him, having an effect similar to a prejudice or an unjustified expectation that does not permit one to see the other in the right light.[10] In general, the question is whether man's religious disposition is in accord with the manifestation of God, whether the primordial religious in man is confirmed by Christ, whether spontaneous piety can find access to Christianity without having to undergo a change.

The question is doubtful for two reasons: first, experience shows us that the conversion to Christ, particularly among religious-minded men, requires conversion of the natural religious instinct; second, it is frequently observed in pastoral care that the natural religious instinct can get out of control and can actually dominate an individual or a parish, creating a situation of strong resistance to the pastor's endeavor toward confrontation with the Gospel and the discernment of the Christian idea. It can even cause so much "irritation" among pious people that it stamps a vivid impression of opposition

[9] "The stronger, or, in any case, the more consistent influence is proper not to conscious but to unconscious attitudes; thus little is done with intellectual instruction and a correction of the conscious attitude." Romano Guardini, *Religion und Offenbarung* (Würzburg, 1958), I, 215.

[10] "It is possible that I completely misunderstand someone who lives before my eyes, because a mysterious will wills it," *ibid.*, p. 214.

between religious nature and the Christian idea.[11] There are
many examples: pretty-looking images of God; magic use of
religious articles; Pharisaic self-righteousness resulting from
prepersonal, quantitative thinking applied to the Christian
idea; the unhealthy asceticism of spiritualistic striving for perfection; excessive feminine attitudes;[12] rejection of the sinner
and discrimination against the sexual, based on a certain idea
of purity; dehumanization of priests by restricting their activi-
ties and lives to pious reactions; reduction of eschatology to
heaven and hell, and many others.

The roots of these and similar influences in the religious
life of both individuals and parishes are too deep and universal to be reached by mere symptomatic treatment. The natural religious disposition takes possession of Revelation and
the figure of Christ and attempts to reduce them to the natural
level, thus blocking the way to the Christian idea. Many pastors get discouraged in their struggle with such groups.[13]

The priest meets this contradiction also in modern varieties
presented in an emphatically religious guise. In the name of
reverend reserve in regard to the impenetrable mystery, one
opposes activism in the Church; in the name of love of fellow
man, one opposes inflexible dogmas; for the sake of a personal
relationship with God, one opposes mass religion; in the name
of individual religion, one opposes collective religion. But a
recent variety is the attitude of some psychotherapists who—

[11] One could say: "Jesus hinders man from living out of the full
religious originality of his interior and of the numinous fullness of the
world. . . . He not only unveils religion but also becomes a 'sign that
shall be contradicted' (Luke 2:34). To every spontaneous piety Christ
first answers 'No,' " Romano Guardini, Die Offenbarung (Würzburg,
1940), p. 890.

[12] The Christian Creed says "Credo in patrem omnipotentem," and
not ". . . in matrem omnipotentem."

[13] It "is part of the Christian's difficult task to defend the Lord not
only against those who reject Him but also against the unenlightened
faithful." Romano Guardini, Religion und Offenbarung, p. 97.

while maintaining that activation of the religious disposition is part of a healthy functioning psyche, and that religion as a method of psychotherapy must be taken very seriously—claim that religion is only a psychological phenomenon; that it depends on the structure of one's inner life whether God exists for the individual;[14] that the kind of religion formulated in the so-called confessional religious keeps man from following the impulses of his heart and from abandoning himself to the fullness of the divine.

c) This shows us that religion and Christianity are to be considered neither as container and content nor as enemies on principle. Their relationship is unbalanced, ambivalent. On the one hand, the religious disposition is necessary in order to grasp the numinous quality of Christ (its proper place in proclamation should be of most concern), and on the other hand it reacts to Christ with simultaneous acceptance and rejection. It may be that man's age-old searching for religion has led it in a wrong direction, that confusions have crept in and obscured it.[15] The religious disposition is both a great help and a great danger for Christian faith. It simply cannot

---

[14] Cf. Olov Hartman, *Holy Masquerade* (Grand Rapids, 1963). The main figure of the novel, the wife of a minister, writes in her diary about her visit with a psychiatrist, of whom she asks: "Do you believe that God exists?" He replies that he is not competent to answer such questions. But he advised it would be good if she could realize her inner religiosity, and that this is something that falls within his competence. He says: "If I could become a happy individual through faith, I should strive for this solution. . . ." Questions of faith and of doubt are treated as "psychological items."

[15] "The development of the religious movement (of mankind) is confused . . . the law of an up and down . . . the last impression is one of a deep futility, not to say, desolation. The high is side by side with the low, the free is side by side with the fearful, the authentic side by side with the vulgar. . . . It is as if something is helplessly seeking, almost finding, then again losing, going astray, starting anew. A great sadness is in the history of the religion of mankind" (Romano Guardini, *Religion und Offenbarung*, p. 45 ff.).

"organically develop into a Christian idea,"[16] but it must be redeemed. If, however, it is included in the process of conversion, in the *metanoia,* it becomes a fertile soil, an ontic ground for the life of faith.

d) The above theologically recognized varieties of the opposition of *sarx*[17] against the invasion of the *pneuma* create great difficulties for the pastor in religious discussions with individuals outside the parish, but even more so within the parish where the opposition is more difficult to be pinned down. In both cases, the difficulties range from a simple deafness and inability of communication to annoyance with scandalizing, unreligious demands that are such a disturbance. This does not astonish those who know the Gospel. It is also obvious that this clash between natural religious disposition and Revelation is unavoidable, and that grace is invisibly effective in this situation, nevertheless, one should try to understand what man's task is in this process.

First, the priest is asked to discern the Christian idea, that is, to know how to differentiate natural religion from religion based on Revelation. The ability of individual diagnosis, as with the physician, rests on knowledge coupled with experience. Knowledge is in our case the knowing of the Revelation, and experience is, more exactly, spiritual experience. The latter is a very characteristic, increasingly more reliable sensitivity to the Christian authenticity or nonauthenticity of religious manifestations, comparable to an experienced ear that intuitively and with seismographic exactitude registers whether the word of a friend is true or not. "But the spiritual man judges all things" (I Cor. 2:15) is realized to the extent of

[16] Cf. Thomas Ohm, *Die Liebe zu Gott in den vorchristlichen Religionen* (Freiburg, 1950), p. 462.

[17] "Sarx," according to St. Paul, is understood as everything distant from God, everything hostile against God within man; man outside the *pneuma,* influenced by the forces of disaster. Cf. Otto Kuss's essay, "Fleisch und Geist," in *Römerbriefkommentar, Regensburger Neues Testament,* 6, (1940), 70 ff.

one's familiarity with the reality of Christ as Man and as the Son of God, of Christ as the Good Shepherd and the Lord of the Cosmos. In spite of the abundance of possible statements and individual manifestations of life there is an extremely sharp dividing line between natural religion and Christian idea when they meet. The fact that natural religious expression is often linked with the very best intentions often renders a "transformation"[18] difficult. Usually it needs a push, even a scandal; more likely such well-intentioned natural religion is so impermeable to the Word of Revelation that this apparently unshakable resistance, coupled at times with an attitude of indolence, seems to be insuperable. Such an attitude, when displayed in some parishes by groups set in their ways, can demoralize the pastor and make him give in or even swing to the side. "One must be happy that the people have good, pious intentions even though they never grasp the Christian idea."

Pastoral care for the "weak" is a separate chapter in the life of the Church[19] and has nothing to do with the mandate to proclaim the true and unabridged Gospel. A guideline for this is the proclamation and the celebration of the Church year.

e) The homily confronts our life with the life of Jesus. A new, exemplary mode of life is presented to us—inviting, urging, even warning. When this presentation takes place on the moral plane, it touches consciousness without converting the religious disposition lying beneath it; and when this disposition is alive, it forms its own religious expression apart from the Gospel. The homily should reach man's depth, for the life and the figure of Jesus appeals not merely to the conscious.

The typically human religious sensitivity should be called to awareness and confronted with Revelation.

[18] Theoderich Kampmann calls it "theologische Überführung" in his book, *Glaube und Erziehung* (München, 1961).

[19] See Chap. XIII in this book.

To speak of human things so that man feels himself understood, to point out the uncertainty of these things and to stimulate man's desire of questioning so that he can become receptive to the answers of the Gospel—are the prerequisites of preaching (steps that are functionally interlinked). Strangely enough, less important aspects, such as sociological changes and differences between the sexes and the age-levels, often play the main role in discussions about preaching. These aspects affect the color and the tone, but they are not concerned with the essence of the question. Only seldom is the most important fact brought into focus, namely, the religious reaction of human nature to Revelation. The theory of preaching —homiletics—needs an anthropological deepening.

f) Proclamation is, first and foremost, a matter of salvation and conversion, and not primarily advice concerning current problems. The purpose of the homily is not to serve the interests of the faithful but to help the faithful become interested in the plans of God. These plans are *universally valid* and address human nature in typical situations: the family, salvation and damnation, illness, death, rebirth, judgment, marriage, pain and suffering, piety.

Take the family, for instance. Today father, mother, children—in short, listeners of all age groups—display a neuralgic reaction toward it. Though thoroughly convinced of the family as basis of society, they still suffer from the restrictions and hazards inherent in it and *expect* Revelation to be a religious protection. Yet, whenever the Gospel speaks about the family, it shows a new constriction of the family based on Christian facts ("Son, why has thou done so to us? Behold, in sorrow thy father and I have been seeking thee." "I have come to bring a sword, not peace." "For I have come to set a man at variance with his father, and a daughter with her mother." "Blessed is the womb that bore thee, and the breasts that nursed thee"). Christianity gives the family a relative character. What a shock for all who prefer to see the family in an air of religious consecration! The foundation of the family is shaken. Contradiction and insight are in strife with each other. How distorted the image of the good Son of God as presented here! He is not at all the gentle humane friend of man that He is thought to be. A preconceived notion makes it hard to see Him as He is. A projection conceals His reality, similar to the projection of Anima and Animus on the beloved.[20] The image of the Son of God, psychologically conceivable within the archetype "savior," is an organ of the natural religious disposition. This archetypal image, with all its expectations, is projected onto Christ; but Christ acts otherwise, and thus the archetype has to be corrected. The insight into the notion of a "different" Jesus causes a dissolution of the projection, with all its unpleasant feelings, and opens one's eyes to the true image of Christ. If, with the assistance of yearly reorientation based on the proclamation of the Gospel, and with conscious persistent effort, this revision is accepted, then a transformation of the natural religious organ also occurs, influencing the primordial image of the Son of God.

And as other themes undergo the same process, there will be a gradual transformation of the religious disposition through a kind of purifying action. Confrontation with Revelation "makes straight" that which was confused. The countenance of God, of Christ, becomes visible, and He is no longer blocked by projections. Facing Christ, the human person is called to a decision: surrender to the divine Person, or follow his own religious instinct. The so-called process of conversion embraces many such revisions; the reorientation of *metanoia* is demanded not only of the conscious, but also of the religious dispositions of the unconscious.

A second example: The Savior, the *Ecce Homo*—the Son of God confronted with the crucified—is another concept that is in need of revision. Habitual thinking must be overcome and the unconscious contradiction made conscious.

[20] See above, p. 112.

A kind of preconceived attitude is the spiritualized notion of the Kingdom of Heaven. The Son of God is seen, with very strong religious expectations, as the leader toward the purely spiritual. He is expected to lead us to heaven, a kingdom of the pure spirits, and to liberate us from the world, from the body and from everything material. Instead the Son of God brings the message of the "Kingdom of God." Whereas Jesus Christ in His time had fought against expectations that were too materialistic, today's preacher, when he speaks about the reality of the Kingdom of God, meets disbelief, anger and surprise. The archetype "heaven" must become relative! Nothing is more difficult than to lead a parish from Good Friday on to a true spirit of Resurrection and Easter joy. While a simple, pious mind can still easily understand that Christ has risen from the dead and that He suffers no longer, Resurrection proclaimed as universal goal is hardly ever assimilated. Only after long, patient, repeated entreaties on the part of the pastor, some will wake up and see the true Savior and Redeemer, thus experiencing the great liberation—the full view of salvation in the Kingdom of God. Hereby the priest can observe the gradual spiritual growth of his parish. But he is also filled with ever new amazement at the sudden joy of a convert, a joy that only the grace of the Holy Spirit can give.

g) The foregoing examples allow us to recognize the following elements in the process of conversion:

(1) Universally human concepts and images are involved (the family, heaven). They have a typical character and have at all times been rooted in the ground of humanity. Corresponding to these are "organs" of the unconscious, known in depth psychology as the archetypal basis. When activated these archetypes[21] enter consciousness in the form of effective primordial images. They are elements of experience, comparable

---

[21] Cf. Jolande Jacobi, *Complex, Archetype, Symbol in the Psychology of C. G. Jung* (New York, 1959).

to "coal-beds containing the energies of entire vegetations, ripening energies of age-old wisdom and insight."[22] They are psychic organs for the perception of corresponding contents and situations of the outer world and are common to all men. Among them we find archetypes related to the numinous-religious, for instance, the divine Child, the Savior, God, daimon, heaven, hell, which assume manifold forms and representations in the myths and religions of all nations.[23] Together they form the natural religious disposition. In religious education, the psychological concept of archetypes should be replaced with the broader and more liberal concept of primordial images,[24] since these images correspond in part to the key concepts of the Bible.[25] The use of primordial images activates the archetypal basis of the religious disposition. This disposition in no way reacts to abstract theological concepts, but only to figurative thinking, which does not correspond to traditional theology but rather to Revelation, to the thinking of salvation history, and of its fruit, kerygmatic theology.

(2) It follows that these activated primordial images are projected onto Christ and His message, and are experienced as anticipation. Thus there is constant danger that the Chris-

[22] Cf. Herzog-Dürck, "Die Behandlung der Neurose als existentielles Problem," in *Psyche*, I, (1947), p. 17.

[23] Since there is no compilation or consistent elaboration of the religious archetypes, we may refer to the following monographs: C. G. Jung & Karoly Kerenyi, *Introduction to a Science of Mythology* (London, 1951); Karoly Kerenyi, *Töchter der Sonne* (Zürich, 1944); Karoly Kerenyi, *The Gods of the Greeks* (New York, 1951). The European and non-European figures of gods reveal the natural religious disposition. Pictures, such as Mathias Grünewald's temptation of St. Anthony and creations of Hieronymus Bosch are attempts to represent the archetypal basis of the religious idea.

[24] Cf. Josef Goldbrunner, "Urbilder—Schlüsselbegriffe—Archetypen," in *Katechetische Blätter* (January, 1964), pp. 1–6.

[25] Cf. Mircea Eliade, *Images and Symbols* (New York, 1961). This work illustrates the extent to which archetypes are rooted in myths. It would be well to differentiate these roots so that the elements of the archetypes could be clearly enucleated.

tian concept is leveled down to one's own view. Christ Himself is hidden behind projections. Even if a natural piety takes a hold on Christ, it nevertheless does not yet permit a faith-instilling encounter.

(3) Therefore, a discernment of the Christian idea should carefully invoke and make conscious the most currently and presently predominant primordial images in order to confront them with their fulfillment in Christ. This means: clear distinctions where necessary, the straightening out of biases and the rejection of errors; but it also means to establish a direct relationship between them wherever possible. Proclamation should confront the primordial images with biblical images, the so-called key-concepts of salvation history.

(4) Careful discernment of the Christian idea leads to the dissolution of unwarranted projections, so that the view of Christ becomes free and a true encounter can take place. Every single correction can make visible a part of Christ's reality. One touches divine reality as if suddenly being dashed against primeval rocks. To the degree that the repetition of the Church year effects such reorientations, sometimes very easily and at times under great strain, the person of man and the Person of the Son of God confront each other.

(5) The stress of this confrontation[26] activates the fourth structural side of the human person. The increasingly liberated view of the Son of God makes possible a spiritual *personal* contact with the divine Person and thus a transcendence beyond the human world into a true encounter with God. The fact that the human person becomes capable of meeting the divine Person in a true encounter reveals a structural side of the person: he is *capax Dei,* capable of grasping God, conforms to Him in his *personalness* and is able to participate in Him.

The frightening experience of meeting the reality of God

---

[26] About the "stress" of this confrontation see Bollnow, *Existenzphilosophie und Pädagogik* (Stuttgart, 1949), p. 99.

Himself as a living Person who speaks and calls and has His own ideas—this possibility and capability awakens the person in its deepest core and ripens its actualization into full *personalness:* everything material, pre*personal,* is incorporated into the *personal;* the person opens his eyes. He is called by his essential "name" in the confrontation with the divine Person. Concisely it means that through the confrontation with the Gospel, the divine Person of Christ calls forth the human person. The human person is awakened to further actualize himself and thus to become capable of grasping the Person of Christ, but also to freely decide for or against Him. Through the "Yes" to the Person of Christ faith is founded.

h) The encounter with the Person of Christ has an effect on the other three structural sides of the human person: first, the significance of one's own existence is realized in the confirmation of the right-of-existence before Christ, who does not dissolve one's identity but rather respects it through the mode of encounter. Secondly, the dialogical mode of being grows into a realistic alertness by one's being allowed to be a partner in conversation. Christ does not overpower, but, through his becoming-Man, creates the distance that permits a dialogue. Thirdly, the experience of creatureliness finds the offering of a Savior who, in His solidarity with entire mankind, heals the roots of our beginning through His death and His descent into the "underworld" and who, in His resurrection, places the image of salvation before our eyes.

i) A new view of the four structural sides of the life of the human person can give an insight into its nature:

> Significance of one's own existence
> Dialogical mode of being
> Creatureliness
> *Capacitas Dei*

The actualization of each structural element leads to the experience of a precondition for the life of faith:

> Right-of-existence before God
> Partnership with God
> Need of salvation
> Transcendence

These are the real and existential experiences and in their totality are called adulthood, maturity or *personal* life.

j) Maturity implies self-control, the capacity for decision, and also responsibility. Here the responsible decision for or against Christ is made. Faith is the fruit of a positive decision, and this leads to the following consequences:

(1) Education and guidance toward the actualization of the person is preparatory to faith, it is an exercise for its realization. For the Christian, grace is not placed high above nature but rather the divine wants to be incarnated in the human. The orientation to human nature, to the anthropological, is therefore a necessary step toward fruitful pastoral care and Christian education.

(2) While the faithful encounter with Christ may become ever more intensive, it will nevertheless remain concealed until the open confrontation with Him in death. The full actualization of the person, for which the Christian strives during his life—and thus the final maturity for decision—can take place only in death.[27]

(3) This exposes the process of maturing to dynamics based on the following phenomena: age-levels of man; sin; and the relationships between mature and immature human beings. This necessarily implies further reflection.

---

[27] Ladislaus Boros bases his book, *The Mystery of Death* (New York, 1965), on this thesis. It is questionable whether this book sees the capacity of personal decision during life as much too relative and the decision in death as almost absolute.

PART THREE

RAMIFICATIONS

CHAPTER XI

Faith and the Various Age-Levels of Man

I N THIS DISCUSSION of the various age-levels of man we are not primarily interested in the details of psychological development,[1] but rather in a synopsis of all the ages of man, so as to gain an insight into the relationship between unfolding human nature and the growth of faith. In this context, too, the development of human nature paralleling the different age-levels is the prerequisite for a progressive incarnation of the Christian idea.

This procedure joins the ascending-descending curve of the biological line with the ascending arrow of the spiritual line

---

[1] Concerning the details of the development of childhood and youth, cf. Heinz Remplein, *Die Entwicklung des Menschen* (München, 1958). Education—including religious education—generally stops short with the psychology of childhood and adolescence, which is understandable, since the educator works with these ages. Faith and Christianity, however, are first related to the adult: only an insight into the whole allows an educational conclusion in regard to the religious possibility of children and adolescents. This leads to practical consequences for the work with the "cosmos of ages" in a parish as well as in religious instruction.

—the ascending arrow indicating the growth of human nature up to its fullness in old age.

The conscious acceptance of each age-level opens up ever new horizons for the realization of faith. Achieving maturity means not only to gain more insight into the doctrine of faith but also to approach truth and to incarnate it in one's own being. Thus there is a correlation between the different age-levels and the insight into faith. Their relationship allows a symbiosis of the dynamics of faith and the possibilities of its realization.

Besides the biological growing and unfolding of human nature, the actualization of the person, too, is related to the different age-levels. Even though there is an interlinking among the tasks of discovering the I, the Thou, the We and God, each nevertheless seems to be specific to a particular stage of growth.

An understanding of the various age-levels is of great help to pastoral activity. The entire life of the faithful is entrusted to the pastor and, if he learns to understand the characteristic dynamics of the different stages and the transition of one to the other, he will avoid making demands that are either premature or long overdue for a certain age group. The biological process pushes man inevitably and instinctively from one age-level to the next, forcing consciousness to adopt an attitude toward it. The precocious child, the infantile six-footer, the Don Juan as the eternal youth, the synthetically rejuvenated —such are the types frequently presenting religious difficulties. But the balance between spiritual attitude and chronological age, the harmony between what should be and what is, awakens one to the truth concerning a specific experience of life and its incarnation. Thus a consciously developed attitude toward a particular age-level can both further one's maturity and help along the incarnation of the Christian concept.

1.

The following survey follows an old classical tradition[2] of five age groups of fourteen (seven times two) years:

1–14 *pueritia*—childhood
14–28 *adolescentia*—youth
28–42 *juventus*—young manhood
young womanhood
42–56 *virilitas*—mature manhood
mature womanhood
56–... *senectus*—old age

Although these divisions are only approximate points of orientation for any particular individual, there are nevertheless two age-levels beginning at 14 and at 56 that are especially changing in our time. The first is the period of adolescence, which, roughly averaged out for both sexes, begins at about the age of 14. There may exist, however, a wide span between physical and psychic development. A child's physical development may be so accelerated that he enters the stage of puberty as early as 10, while at the same time his psychic development may lag three or four years after 14. Such situation causes a sexual awareness and capability incommensurate with the child's psychic responsibility. Moral judgment must take this into account. Whereas the transition stage at 14 is a period of crisis in religious education, the change at 56 causes no such difficulty, for in modern times it seems to be postponed to the point where even a sociological change can be observed in the structure of human society. While some one hundred years ago (1850) statistics put the average age of the European at

---

[2] Cf. Hans Künkel, *Die Lebensalter* (Konstanz, 1957); see also Romano Guardini, *Die Lebensalter* (Würzburg, n.d.).

35, life-expectancy today has increased 100 per cent to the age of 70. The reason for this is progress in civilization and medical science, which in turn resulted in an extended period of *virilitas* and a postponement of the well-known change at 56,[3] the "great age crisis."

2.

A description of the characteristic traits of each age-level shows a progressive unfolding of human nature to an ever greater humanness. Each age has different functions, the performance of which is made possible by the development of human nature. These tasks are, so to speak, the vital material with which the Christian confronts religious facts in order to grasp their meaning. Thus there is a parallel between the vitality of a specific age-level and the realization of the truths of faith. Once their correlation is recognized and considered in pastoral care, a mutual understanding becomes possible, setting up a bond of trust between pastor and faithful.

3.

In order to accept the individual age-levels it is of crucial importance to go through the age-crises—the transitions from one stage to another. True, the so-called old age crisis, generally the only recognized crisis, is the most difficult; but the transitions at 14, 28 and 42 are likewise crises having characteristic effects, dangers and opportunities. The crisis of puberty at the age of 14 should not obscure the difficulties of the other transitions.

The transition at each age-level is a crisis with definite phases. The process can be compared to the developmental

[3] We are flooded with books on gerontology (15,000) concerning the sociological consequences of this shifting of the pyramid of ages in modern society. To name just two: Ernst Michel, *Der Prozess "Gesellschaft contra Person"* (Stuttgart, 1959), pp. 215–246; "Gerontologie," in *Der Grosse Herder,* XI, col. 717–728.

stages of the chrysalis of a caterpillar: (a) the caterpillar begins to spin its cocoon; (b) a period of inactivity follows; seen from the outside, the chrysalis appears lifeless; (c) interiorly new powers are growing. Unnoticeably something new is forming; (d) the new form breaks through the cocoon and the old is left behind; (e) the new form of life, the butterfly, tests its powers and unfolds them into new life. All these phases are experienced in the age crises and can be interpreted psychologically as follows:

a) An inner restlessness releases one from the life-form of the present age-level.

b) A period of inactivity follows, which is experienced as inability to cope with oneself and with the world. One is disorientated, unable to make decisions; it is as if all energies are withdrawn from consciousness. This lack of orientation may be experienced as depression.

c) Vital powers are active in the inner realm; one's energies are withdrawn into the unconscious, are "in the womb," where the new form is being prepared. Any conscious effort to draw out energy from this inner process of becoming interferes with and slows down the interior event and, therefore, the educator must be patient with the disorientation of the child passing through the crisis of puberty.

d) More or less suddenly the bound up forces are set free and are once more at the disposal of consciousness; and again one can begin to act, but now turning to new interests and tasks. Former relationships are either dissolved (childhood friendships often end with adolescence) or undergo a change (the difference in the child's attitude toward the educator after entering puberty, or in the relationship between husband and wife at the crises of 28 and 42). The relinquishing of old relationships is like the abandoning of an empty cocoon, the shedding of an old skin. If the new phase of life is not understood by others and the present environment does not participate in this development, it may seem like a kind of infidelity.

For often one goes on ahead, while the others lag behind or even stop short. It is a continuous source of life—changes, difficulties, misunderstandings and new possibilities in human society—observable not only in the individual but also collectively, a fact that is particularly evident in mission work with its different groups, tribes, nations and cultural levels.

e) A new vitality is assimilated; a new rhythm fills life; the step becomes more firm and new tasks are assumed. A new man appears. Glancing backward and comparing pictures of one's childhood with those of adolescence, or pictures of young manhood with those of mature manhood, one is often amazed at the obvious change.

Fairy tales and myths are dramatic expressions of psychic crises. Take, for instance, *Hansel and Gretel*. The child is kept in a cage by the witch (the personified, dangerous, unknown future, endowed with mysterious forces). The child is helpless, and only inwardly can his strength increase; the witch herself helps him to grow stronger. Finally, with his sister's help, he is strong enough to escape from the cage. (What is meant here is not wifely but sisterly help, meaning one's own fellow man with his advice and active help.) Then he changes into his new life and burns the witch, that is, he suddenly overcomes the danger.

Another representation of this transition in a crisis is found in the myth of the whale-dragon.[4] The hero is swallowed by the monster (in other versions the leviathan or the ocean swallows him). In the stomach of the animal he gets nourishment (some myths say that he ate its heart). He is then disgorged. Of course, this myth is primarily an analogy to the outer world: each day the sun goes down into the ocean and rises out of it again. But, in a mystic participation, the inner process is related to the outside event. Through the projection of the inner process, both events are parallel. What is observed

[4] Cf. Leo Frobenius, *Das Zeitalter des Sonnengottes* (Berlin, 1904).

of the sun becomes the dramatized symbolic expression of the inner experience of crisis: the lord of consciousness, the *I,* is swallowed by the unknown and by the dangerous forces of the unconscious (all energies are withdrawn into the unconscious). Man in a crisis is as if paralyzed, incapable of decision. Inside, however, in the unconscious a change is taking place, and with the forces of the unconscious a new orientation is found; the energies surge once more toward consciousness, and the *I* finds the power of resolution and decision.

All three analogies, the cocoon, the fairy tale and the myth, permit an insight into the psychic events occurring in an age-crisis and give an idea of the difficult tasks that have to be solved within one's self. During this period of personal confusion religious commitment can provide support. But it can also happen that the religious factor itself is drawn into the whirlpool of changes (generally the case today). The pastor should know how to be an understanding counselor. In so far as he is aware of the nature of the next age-level and of the human and religious difficulties of transition, he will confidently await the moment of maturing and disregard the temporary disbelief as a mere symptom of the inner crisis, and not as something final.

We will now describe the individual age-levels of man, characterize the crisis of each transition and outline their consequences for the Christian life.

4.

Two tasks are assigned to the period of *childhood,* one is exterior and the other interior. The home and school prepare the child for community and help toward integration into community life. In the home, the primary foundation of community, the child learns how to walk and talk; he is also trained in proper behavior, hygiene and table manners, thus becoming prepared to take his place in society. The school addresses the powers of consciousness, develops the skills of reading, writing and calculating, thus providing training in the habits of civilized life. One is never better in mental arithmetic and memorizing than at about the age of 12. In this period the main psychological function of consciousness is to learn in a purely formal way how to think. It is possible to provide a fundamental experience of community in a well-managed class room by the practice of social behavior in the form of mutual consideration and help. Social education provides the tools for the tasks of life, for the traffic of man. Symbol for this age-level is *Mercury,* the messenger of the gods. "In the tenth year Mercury reigns. Like him, man moves rapidly and easily, in the smallest circle; he can be influenced by little things; but it is easy for him to learn many things under the dominion of the god of subtlety and eloquence."[5]

In the religious sphere, too, the child is introduced into relationships, into an association with the "above." He listens to biblical stories and learns the catechism. A family life rooted in faith, along with a living parish and school, integrates the child into the life of Christian community through training and example. He acquires the material for his later decision of faith; his Christian form of life is like a container that is being prepared so that it can later be filled with a Christian life born of his own decision. A child's interior task, however, is the more difficult. Child psychology generally speaks only about the phenomena of external behavior, but these are merely the symptoms of a much more important interior event taking place in the unconscious or at the borderline between the conscious and unconscious, which is one's integration into the development of mankind, into its history. Goethe, who was well versed in human nature, says that the child "must pass through the epochs of world-culture";[6] he must, in these

---

[5] Schopenhauer in an aphorism, quoted by Künkel, in *Die Lebensalter,* p. 31.

[6] Cf. Goethe, *Conversations with Eckerman* (Washington, 1901).

14 years, live through many centuries. This is a great achievement causing much internal stress. This amusing description offers an insight into the inner process of the age of childhood.

"The cave man under the table or couch develops into a hunter and collector who picks flowers and collects butterflies. He grows into a happy shepherd in the meadow and into the first farmer. In his first street fights he lives through the wild times of the migration of nations and becomes deeply engrossed in his history books with the dedication of a monk of the early Middle Ages. A young hero and knight at the age of 12, he joins the Crusaders, and finds himself in violent religious arguments as soon as he reaches the age of the Reformation. At the start of his teens he fights the thirty years' war against each and everyone in his destructive attitude toward the values of his childhood and often, also, the appearance of his own home. Only then modern man with his organization of work and his specialized knowledge begins to wake up within him and he decides which profession he will choose as an apprentice of the present day."[7]

Such re-experiencing of the "phylogenesis in ontogenesis" certainly does not happen consciously, but is more like a lengthy *dream*. It manifests itself in the conscious through symbolic forms of living that parallel the above-mentioned epochs. Educational influences at home and school should adjust to this instinctive process of a gradual approach to the present and not interfere with it by straining the conscious through "overexposure." Overworking the conscious would draw too much energy from the unconscious and cause a precocious conscious. But in this case it would not be sustained by a healthy, safe underground.[8] A gradual, organismic approach is needed, for instance, reading material corresponding to the developmental stage of the child would be of great help in furthering healthy development.

[7] Cf. Künkel, *Die Lebensalter*, p. 61.
[8] For example, taking the children on a trip to foreign countries; but the acquired world-view hardly compensates for the superficial sophistication resulting from their lack of capacity for realization.

Religion is closely connected with this "dream-life." The events in Bible stories and in the lives of saints are experienced by the child, at times even intensively, but they are not yet related to the core of man that still lies dormant. The *person* is not yet actualized. Even so, it is most important that the ground of the soul come in contact with religious stories and holy deeds. Momentary *personal* actions of the child become possible only by participating in the faith of adults. The key-figures of childhood, father, mother, grandparents, as well as teachers and catechists, sustain the religious life of the children. Whatever *they* love, the child will love and do. His faith is a faith of obedience, his ethics an ethics of obedience.[9] The faith acquired during the first fourteen years of life is not able to sustain its new situation of apprenticeship, not even in high school, unless religious life is supported and guided by youth groups.

Therefore, a parish that is mainly orientated to pastoral care for children can easily slip into self-deception. Since it is not difficult to lead a group of children into religious activity, a priest talented in pastoral care for children can easily make it flourish through the skillful use of pedagogical techniques and a little pressure, but this is no yardstick for the actual faith of a parish. Pastoral care for children can, at best, be only a preconditioning for a positive, and today generally indispensable, future *decision* of faith. Thus, even though childhood and adolescence are important for the decision of faith, the main accent of pastoral care must be placed on the adults.

Here we can describe childhood in the following schema:

1–14—childhood—pueritia—thinking—Mercury—dream

---

[9] Cf. Michael Pfliegler, *The Right Moment* (Notre Dame, 1966); Theodor Müncker, *Psychologische Grundlagen der Katholischen Sittenlehre* (Düsseldorf, 1953), p. 114; J. A. Jungmann, *Handing on the Faith* (New York, 1959).

5.

Every dream leads to an awakening—childhood ends with disillusionment. The *I*, which before puberty hardly plays a role in life,[10] opens its eyes and, in a first discovery of its identity, emphatically seeks to hold on to its differentiation. It sees the world realistically and critically, no longer under the influence of the dream. Such disillusionment leads his confidence in his parents, the "first educators,"[11] into crisis. One could express the experience of the adolescent thus: "The world is different from what you told me; it is harder, more hostile. You deceived me." Naturally this is only a projection onto the educators of an inner event that is not understood. Here it is not the educator's task to try to maintain the former relationship, but to understand this distrust as a symptom and to step back. Often the influence of parents is pushed into the background by the school chaplain or a teacher, the so-called secondary educators. Rather than try to force their students to have confidence in them, educators and teachers should refer such a group or class to someone else. For in this crisis of puberty educational influence is possible only in connection with a freely given confidence that is not so much founded in the conscious but rather has sympathy as its emotional basis.

The cocoon-phase deprives the youngsters of the possibility of orientating themselves, and, therefore, they often escape into a peer-dominated society that forms gangs. The only thing they share together is their inner confusion and their aggressive attitude toward the environment. Every Hansel has been caught by the witch and thrashes around in his cage.

But one day a force breaks through, creating a new possibility of contact with the world. The adolescent listens to

[10] Cf. Wilhelm Hansen, *Die Entwicklung des kindlichen Weltbildes* (München, 1965).

[11] Cf. Heinrich Kahlefeld, "Der erste, zweite, dritte Erzieher," in *Katechetische Blätter* (April, 1954), pp. 129–132.

music and feels that he has never heard music before. He looks at a landscape as though seeing it for the first time. He sees the face of a girl and she haunts his dreams. Eros—the capacity of establishing a loving relationship to everything worthwhile—has awakened a psychic power that gives the world a new touch. Youth sets enthusiasm on fire; thought is no longer the paramount function, but *feeling* takes the lead over all the other psychic powers.

Feeling, however, is a typically feminine function. Thus, in adolescence, the feminine sex is instinctively superior and more mature than the masculine. Girls find their way back sooner than the boys; when they are seventeen they already look the way they are intended to be, while the boys still move around as though put together in unco-ordinated segments. Both have the task to integrate the enthusiastic powers of Eros in their associations with beauty, value, goodness, truth, art and religion, especially through the formation of the life of love and sex. *Venus* dethrones Mercury. The life of youth is no longer a dream but now becomes a *melody*.

The halfway point of adolescence, the twenty-first year (comparable to the crisis of the seven-year-old who has just started school) supposedly has reached the "age of reason." From now on youth is expected to exercise a certain control over emotions and is considered by the State fully capable of legal rights and obligations. Of course, the number "twenty-one" is only an approximation, for legal majority does not always indicate full maturity in all areas of life—think of marriage, for instance. Likewise we should certainly ask the question "What is the age of a truly mature decision for or against the faith, and what are the contributions of the first seven years of adolescence to this decision?"

The enthusiastic powers of Eros render relationships with the surrounding world more intensive than they could ever be in later years, but, like the melody of a song, they have their highs and lows. Even though in our prosaic times they no longer swing to the extremes of "rejoicing to the highest heavens and grieving unto death," to temporary submission, to the undulating movement of up and down, to the blooming and dying of a relationship—nevertheless the essential question still arises whether the fluctuation of emotionality can possibly be measured. Their inner world is going through a process of reconstruction, even though the process escapes conscious formulation. The repeated experience of undulation sets up a sense of anticipation: it will happen again, the same as the last time, and the happy feeling will pass and be replaced by a sobering disillusionment; the wave reaches its crest and suddenly declines. The realm of experience is divided: an inner reserve forms itself against the exclusively positive or negative vitality. One part of the inner world attempts to differentiate itself from this vitality and to confront it. Man confronts himself; the *I* begins to free itself from the embrace of feelings and to take a stand regarding them. His attitude may be skeptical, critical, benevolent or hostile, yet he recognizes more and more that the world of feeling undulates along a midline, and that the awareness of this midline gives him orientation.

Growth in this recognition, more subconscious than conscious, creates the possibility of resting within one's self and of finding one's self, and simultaneously leads to the question of the direction and the goal of this midline. This new question "Does liberation from emotional undulation stabilize an individual, so that he can set his sights on another dimension, the movement toward the future?" is not a merely intellectual formulation but rather existential, arising from the inmost core. Individual being itself is in question and constellates the search for meaning on three levels: on the human level where a conscious self-education begins; on the professional level, where career-planning is taking shape; on the religious level, where the decision of faith is drawing near.

Although enthusiasm makes intensive religious experience

possible, and is required for religious decision, this new skepticism strives also for independence in the religious realm by freeing itself from religious sentiment. But this very skepticism can come to life through enthusiasm and give the impetus to live as a Christian, to work in the world as a Christian. It is of utmost importance that the religious decision be directed to the world. The question of the meaning of life, asked for the first time in an existential way, demands a religious answer that does not abandon the world (as in the so-called schema of ascent[12]), but that gives religion a home in the world and thus the world a home in religion. Here the first two characteristics of our salvation-situation[13] become actual: the dimension of future and the hidden presence.

But it is also possible that this existential question of the meaning of life can find only an anti-Christian answer. Rebellious vital energy rejecting every kind of restriction, or a parish lacking a positive view of the world, can easily be the reason. But in every case we must remember that the question of the meaning of life repeatedly presents itself, each time providing the possibility of conversion.

A situation, however, that is not so normal as the above, and yet one that is tending to appear much more frequently, is the awakening of Sexus without concomitant awakening of Eros, or the awakening of an Eros sickened by a cheap, blasé attitude. Then the powers of enthusiasm are strangled, the rhythmic undulations, the highs and the lows, are flattened out, and nothing remains but simmering sex. Religious development dies in this suffocation of psychic development. Human nature is sick, religiously deaf, cheated out of the best part of its youth. The dream of childhood·is not followed by a song; the chrysalis could not mature. The "Hansel" in the cage did not get the food he needed; he refused his sister's help and entered a "pact" with the witch which, while giv-

[12] See above, pp. 11–12.
[13] See above, p. 39.

ing him external freedom, had enslaved him interiorly all
the more.

The understanding of such a condition unburdens the priest
from unnecessary responsibility, and youth from the pressure
of impossible expectations. The priest does not feel that he
has to be on top of every situation, but rather encourages a
type of trusting relationship that represents a golden bridge
for future religious development. Concisely, the following is
the schema for the period of youth:

14–28—youth—adolescentia—feeling—Venus—song

6.

Since feeling is the main psychological function of the age
of youth, it is in this period that the female reaches her peak.
A woman of 24 holding her baby is not only the image of
the madonna, but also a universally human high point in the
life of the woman, as well as the image of the fullness of life.
To descend from this peak at the age of 28 and to enter *young
womanhood* is a most difficult task. The song has come to an
end, as did the dream, and the new way of life is one of prosaic
service. Often the man is not even aware of this transition,
as he goes energetically forward into the new age of *young
manhood* that carries him toward the peak of his manhood.
He changes: exteriorly, he acquires skill in managing others
and strength of will; he tends to harden emotionally. What
he has done before with enthusiasm he now bases on strict
reason; his interests are almost exclusively absorbed by his
profession, which he intends to build up into a position for
life. He uses his capacities systematically. With foresight he
purchases his own home, where his family can have comfort
and security. The ruling function is no longer feeling but *willing;* Venus has abdicated to *Mars,* representing the aggressive
willpower of the soldier and officer on duty—a typical picture
of manliness, which, however, is also obviously one-sided.

The man's intense absorption in his work and profession

forces him to turn toward the world. This is the critical point in the religious development of the age-level of young manhood. If the young man succeeds in seeing the world as creation, and in seeing his professional activity as a co-operative forming of this creation by order of the Creator, this then will not only affect his attitude toward the world but will also ground his work in the Church. The realistic piety of this age-level is expressed, above all, in a prudent dealing with the world, in reliable service and creative activity.[14]

For the woman, however, the transition into such a typically masculine age-level is a difficult task. Externally, it means the beginning of her descent from the peak of physiological development (a fact that tempts many to extend it artificially). Inwardly, however, her task is even more difficult, since she has to integrate a masculine attitude within herself: she must exercise an organizing will and be no longer guided by mere feelings. In marriage this means submission to a daily household routine and each day the surrender to a plan. If a home is to function well, it demands sensible organization; the "lovable" disorder of the time of Venus is no longer permitted; married life becomes service. More or less reluctantly, perhaps, but still consciously, the discipline of Mars must be accepted. The masculine attitude must be integrated with the feminine. To the degree that this integration is realized she has prepared herself to reach the highpoint of the next age-level, *mature womanhood,* after 42.

Unmarried women have similar problems: every day the same routine at the office, or perhaps the drudgery of teaching school. If she does not accept this dull routine and instead tries to root her nature in something outside of it—striving, so to speak, to live her life as a woman independent of her profession—she deprives herself of the opportunity of matur-

---

[14] Cf. Karl Rahner, "Messopfer und Jugendaszese," in *Sendung und Gnade* (Innsbruck, 1959), pp. 166 ff.

ing into a complete human being through the integration of
the masculine and feminine aspects of her life. "Will—Mars—
Service" signify for the woman (married or not) a necessary
transition, which should have taken place at least by the age
of 35, molding her into the *mulier fortis* who is a partner to
man in the service of life.

Often the transition at the age of 28 leads to marriage crises.
Both, for instance, marry during the period of Venus, he at
25, she at 20. Their mode of life together and of being-in-the-
world is characterized by the function of feeling. They are
united like two voices singing in harmony. At about the age
of 28, however, the male partner changes, he becomes prosaic.
He is no longer interested in traveling, music and all the wonderful things of the early years of marriage; he now lives only
for his profession. His theme is no longer the I-Thou relationship; he takes it for granted, as the restful center giving him
strength for his work. But she, still in the age of Venus, feels
neglected, misunderstood, left alone. He makes demands on
her, based on will; but she responds emotionally. Her main
theme is still the I-Thou relationship. The song of their life
is constantly interrupted by the telephone calling him to work.
If they are to stay together, they need good close friends from
whom they learn to understand their own changes. Marriage
guidance should not be limited to exhortations on the indis-
solubility of marriage; as important and generally more
helpful is the explanation of the reasons underlying the development of their relationship. An insight into the age-levels
can reveal that both are maturing toward a deeper mutual
understanding, and that there is the promise of a wonderful
Indian Summer in their marriage—if only they faithfully fulfill the duties of young manhood and young womanhood.
The fruit of this understanding can also be the recognition
that love, Sexus and Eros, are not the only things in the world
worth living for—not even the most important things. Involvement with creation, family life, children, professional

activity, community life, politics—all this is worth living for.

Seen in the light of religion, God entrusts man with His creation. Dealing with it in matters of daily life, in a reliable, loving way, is man's service to it; in fact, it is also man's religious service. The stuff of the world must be spiritually molded, so that man, with faith as his basis, can act in creation as a Christian. Professional activity is the medium through which the divine plans permeate the world.

Again we can summarize the age-level between 28 and 42 as follows:

28–42—virilitas—willing—Mars—service

7.

The next transition at 42 is much more a crisis for the man than for the woman, for she is at this point growing into a new sense of vitality. The man, however, must now descend from his peak of masculinity, that is, from the heights of Mars. He discovers (sooner or later) that he cannot achieve everything with his will; he cannot ram his head through a wall; he cannot preplan, organize, order and command everything. He reacts with resentment, at first with feelings of humiliation and aggravation. He overtaxes his strength, until his failure tells him that at the very point where his will power has failed, a helpful phenomenon can be observed—in other words, that there are developments. The more he is aware of this, the more he learns to estimate these new developments and to put his trust in them. He becomes calmer, more patient; he waits and goes into action only when the time has come. He achieves much more with less energy than he had exerted in his willful aggression.

This *trust* in the development of things becomes the main function, superseding the will. He looks ahead, joins the past with the future and waits—encouraging others, supporting with a word here and there, helping, admonishing. He now understands how human beings must be guided; he can lead and rule. He has entered *mature manhood,* characterized by *Jupiter,* the planet of priests and kings. He no longer merely organizes, no longer merely administrates or makes rules, but reigns. With his help many difficulties in community life recede into their natural perspective, and the people around him react differently, become calmer, for there is something about him that affects them—the dignity of the mature man. This is the age of leadership and direction, the age of assuming responsibility for community life, from a religious point of view as well. Tremendous development has taken place: from the dream to the song to service, and now, as human dignity blossoms, the *throne* becomes the symbol of this age-level of man.

The unfolding of human nature can also be seen by comparing the different main psychological functions: thinking, feeling, willing, trusting. To trust is no longer typically feminine as is feeling, or typically masculine as is willing, but universally human. Trust in the development of things as a guiding and sustaining characteristic is proper to feminine nature and leads the woman to a new peak of mature womanhood. It is also proper to the man in so far as he overcomes his one-sided masculine attitude in his struggle for maturity. Trust as the main psychic function also creates a new possibility of contact between the sexes: they no longer confront each other as *male* and *female* human beings, but as male and female *human beings.* The one-sided masculine vs. the feminine is broadened into humanness; sexual differentiation is part of a greater context, that is, the being a human of masculine or feminine kind; sex serves humanity. Fruit of such a development is the "Indian Summer" in many marriages, and also in many friendships.

The characteristic strength of this age-level, *trust,* represents a natural basis for a definite deepening of faith. Learning to trust in development means to make the experience of time part of the life of faith.

a) Personal experience with developments, allowing things to work out, makes one open to God's acting in time, which religion calls Providence. For instance, all the pressing why-questions (Why did this happen to me? Why did he have to die so young?) are seen in a new dimension. The presentiment of underlying developments makes possible not only an intellectual trust in Providence but also a deeper, existential acceptance.

b) A trusting relationship with the experience of time creates a new understanding of history, an interest in salvation history. The interest in God's great salvific plan broadens faith. The great movement of the world is seen from the viewpoint of salvation history, which in turn results in a deeper understanding of the present salvation-situation with its four elements.[15] A faith that turns toward the world becomes mature.

c) Whoever has witnessed the effectiveness of human maturity in others, or has experienced it in himself, knows what dignity is. This priceless quality of mature humanity permits a presentiment of God's dignity, the dignity of a God who reigns as King and who revealed Himself in Sacred Scripture. God's dignity enriches the image of God.

To sum up:

42–56—virilitas—trust—Jupiter—throne

8.

The transition into old age[16] presents the most difficult task for human development for it means the dethronement of man, against which, at first, all the stuff of human nature rebels. The first signs appear when the new generation wants to move up. The older generation is, of course, proud of the new, since it has produced it, and enjoys its initial successes. The new gen-

---

[15] See above, pp. 39 ff.
[16] We have already dealt with the postponement of the old-age crisis in our day (see p. 165).

eration thinks differently, which is understandable, and keeps one flexible. But the younger generation also feels and senses differently, and this the older generation cannot absorb—not even from the books. A new alien world is springing up! Though still feeling oneself in the fullness of one's years, enjoying the peak of life in the period of Jupiter, and though still making plans for the future, one begins to feel a cold breeze. The young generation moves up and, quite unexpectedly, something like distrust creeps into one's benevolent attitude toward it—the first external sign of the advancing crisis of aging. Interiorly, the chill is felt more deeply: "Life goes on! Is it possible that some day I will be no longer needed?" To anticipate this intellectually while still young is different from being actually touched by it. "But that life could let me drop like an apple from the tree, this does not make sense!" Both reactions, the outward and the inward, unite to cause the specific characteristic of the crisis of aging, which is distrust of the young; the younger generation is the object of elderly people's reaction to the development of life. He who sits on the throne of life seeks to keep it; he will neither give up nor give in, and every attempt of the young to climb higher is nipped in the bud. He becomes extremely angry, like *"Saturn, who devours his own children."*

A typical example of this is the sixty-year-old farmer who refuses to turn over the farm to his thirty-year-old son; as a consequence, the son cannot marry. The father turns against the life of his son and prevents his development; in some part of his being he would like to have the son out of his life, or even desires to kill him: psychologically he devours his own child, in accordance with the exaggerated mythological motif.

The time element of this struggle varies. Often a physical breakdown assists the process; as the biological line declines, life urges toward abdication. Or else a catastrophe with one's fellow workers might develop and force a change, for instance, in the form of a limitation of one's own activity that forces a retirement. Often distrust turns into a fixation. The inner movement concentrates more and more on the question "Does life have meaning, even though it no longer needs me and drops me?" The answer can be worked out in different stages.

a) "If I can no longer work, and the purpose of my life is stolen from me, and if, without any power of resistance left in me, I have no way to defend myself against the others who push me, what can I do but capitulate before this secret conspiracy? Life is hostile, and the only thing left for me is to shift from a losing battle into resignation." Thus he gives up all ambition, makes no more demands, becomes tired and loses vitality: a resigned and mean old man. For many people life at this point comes actually to an end; they die shortly after their retirement.

b) But whoever has lived through all the age-levels in a normal way continues to have a zest for living. Even in the face of resignation the question persists concerning the meaning of life: "In spite of everything, does life really have meaning, independent of myself? Perhaps on the other side?" A change from the visible to the invisible begins to take place, implying the concept of depth. In the background of the great crisis of aging is the coming-to-grips with death even though one no longer talks about it. This coming-to-grips with death is the touchstone by which the power of life, figuratively speaking, is transformed into another form of energy, in the same way that the energy of a waterfall is transformed into electrical power. But since life is not a mechanical but a spiritual process, all the elements of the former phases of life play their part, giving it a forward impetus. Resignation and paralysis are followed by a storm of rebellion and despondency. Attempts at thinking beyond the threshold lead to frightening setbacks and, then, new attempts. All earlier events play a part in this change; every former age-crisis that was not accepted has now a hindering effect, and every age-crisis consciously and fully accepted now proves to be of help. Christian faith, consciously accepted, has a supporting influence, but it does not replace the natural maturing process in the birth pangs of the old-age crisis. One's whole life cries out: Is there something on the other side after death? One's entire nature is a painful question: What will happen at the gate of death? Is there something beyond that sheds light on my present crisis and allows me to grasp its meaning? Suddenly life calms down— nobody knows when—and the tension subsides.

The clarification and purification now experienced can be compared to the fermentation of wine, whereby the dregs are precipitated and the pure wine is formed. Vital energy tends to *believe* that life has a hidden meaning, even if the meaning is not understood. This belief is not an emergency-solution, caused by fear—fear has no sustaining power—since this process of purification is only partly in the conscious, and only partly in the unconscious, finding its decision in the super-conscious realm of the person.

In this state of development a man can step back, not in hostility but in peace with the world, with his successors and with God. His health is restored, and though less robust he now grows old like Uranus, the oldest of all, who now replaces Saturn. He becomes kind and gentle like the mild *winter sun,* the new and last symbol of this age-level. Then it often happens that the younger generation will now approach him for advice, since they no longer need to fear the interference of his subjective ambitions. He has exchanged his throne for the *haven of peace.*

When this *natural* faith is joined to the Christian message, the result is a blossoming life of faith that is described in the Apocalypse (4:10–11): The twenty-four elders (certainly selected leaders, but behind them is the experience and wisdom of life) cast their crowns before the throne of God as though offering the experience and wisdom of their entire life in thanksgiving. This symbolic act finds verbal expression in their prayer: "Worthy art thou to receive glory and honor. . . ."

One could interpret this to mean: "My entire life is the worship of your power and your will." One's whole life becomes a prayer: "Not I but Thou."

This *natural* faith now points in the same direction as does the religious attitude of Christian faith. They go side by side in such way that they can unite and support each other. The human and Christian maturity of the older generation is a lighthouse to the younger, who look to them to find their own orientation. Many an aged priest, bishop or pope is literally a bridge-builder to the other world—they are *pontifices*. Again, specific truths of faith are correlated with this development of the life of faith.

Whoever "departs from this world," who gives his last blessing to the world and adopts a benevolent attitude toward it, lives within the world without being of the world. He realizes the value of created things, but still is not enslaved by them. "He possesses as though he did not possess." The overcoming of the old-age crisis detaches man from nonessentials and opens his eyes to the prophecies of the new heaven and the new earth. The eschatological attitude of St. Paul (I Cor. 7:29–32) is thus achieved by natural sensitivity.

The kindness of old age is not mere naivete but it has become possible in spite of all the sad experiences of life. It is an image of the kindness of God, which also remains the same in spite of all His experiences with mankind. His kindness, too, is not naivete but the expression of His benevolence, His desire to give His blessing to mankind.

Whoever in the natural realm is so strongly pushed toward the borderline between the here and the beyond has also a natural presentiment of the threshold between both realms, which nevertheless is so sharply dividing. It is a "thin wall" built by man from his "images,"[17] which could collapse "without noise or sound" through the "call of a mouth." The Chris-

---

[17] Cf. R. M. Rilke, *Poems from the Book of Hours* (Norfolk, 1941).

tian may interpret this as an experience of God, who is both near and far at the same time. He, the "totally other," beyond all images, is both here and there—two actualities that, in the experience of the threshold, melt into a union like that of coinciding opposites. The believing mind experiences such thoughts as the sheltering action of divine omnipotence. Concisely we can sketch old age as follows:

56— . . . —Senectus—believing—Saturn—haven of peace
Uranus
Sun

9.

A quick look at these five age-levels reveals a continuously ascending movement that is in contrast to the ascending-descending curve of the biological development.[18] This illustration clearly indicates the progressive unfolding of human nature:

dream—song—service—throne—haven of peace
Mercury—Venus—Mars—Jupiter—Saturn—Uranus—Sun.

The psychic disposition characteristic of each age-level also shows that life becomes more and more intensive and human, especially since every previous disposition is preserved and absorbed by the new phase, thus finally leading human nature to full maturity:

thinking—feeling—willing—trusting—believing.

The consequences for Christian life are as follows:

a) The summary of all the age-levels brings into view human nature with all its possibilities of development. Each developmental stage is seen as temporary, and as related to a final goal, thus losing its absolutity. What now becomes interesting is human development viewed in its totality. The

[18] See above, p. 164.

one-sided, fixated view of the biological line of aging is set free for the much more important view of spiritual development. The psyche is not detached from biological facts, but gives them their place in the great context of the human journey through the age-levels. The spiritual movement joins the biological. While psychological resistance to old age hinders the normal biological pattern and affects one's health, a conscious acceptance of the age-levels tends to be psychosomatically constructive.

b) The joy of full human development leads one to seek out mature people who can converse on a level much deeper than that of the usual intellectual conversation. Does this not also shed light on man's relationship with God? Could it mean that God would like to converse with mature men? Is God looking for Christians who have grown up from "children of God" into "sons and daughters" with whom He can dialogue and who understand Him, not merely intellectually but also maturely. It is not too difficult to imagine that the father of the prodigal son was happy that his son now had become mature and understanding, and that he enjoyed talking with him about matters requiring an experience of the world. The mature man as partner in conversation with God broadens the image of God. The image of God is as mature as the maturity of the person who "images" Him. He is the Creator of man who resembles Him. Perfection (Matt. 5:48) means not only ethical perfectness but also human wholeness. This means in practical application that Christian education and self-development should not only be directed toward perfectness but also toward wholeness, the full unfolding of human nature.

c) Remaining fixed at a certain age-level is a failure to fulfill God's expectation. The task God has given us is the unfolding of our nature into wholeness (moral theology terms this self-love). Therefore, since everything created is called to its full flowering, any culpable retardation of development must be made up. This fact sheds light on Purgatory, which is not only a place for the expiation of sin but also a place for man's complete unfolding.[19] The more man is man the more he is *capax Dei:* he fulfills God's expectations, becoming a vis-à-vis partner of God and a part of redeemed mankind destined to mature into the "fullness of Christ" (Eph. 4:13).

d) A consideration of the different age-levels causes man to think beyond himself and his immediate present, and to learn how to see himself in context. The absolute character of the present becomes relative; one sees himself as a part of the great movement of the generations, which flows on unflaggingly. Of course, this interferes with the naive sense of vitality, especially in the young. The simple naivete is lost, but in exchange a greater consciousness is gained. This consciousness is necessary for all who are involved in human guidance: teachers, physicians, psychologists and priests. The training of future teachers and priests should aim at broadening this awareness. The first overfocused, excessively introspective, attitudes of the apprentices will probably be only a transitional phase leading to a deeper understanding of the entire context, which, after a few years of practical experience, will establish a new security. Thus their stability will be based also on a knowledge of man's journey through the various age-levels.

e) The experience of the relativity of the present becomes concrete, when we consider that the present generation will be dismissed in the same manner as has every previous one. Consequently the transitional nature of each generation should be brought into the focus of consciousness.

Everyone is only an element of mankind, and as such he also participates in the salvation of mankind. Christ's salvific act is seen as the "cosmic event," which, of course, every indi-

---

[19] Cf. Otto Betz, "Purgatorium—Reifwerden für Gott," in *Katechetische Blätter* (January, 1957), pp. 15–18; see also Ladislaus Boros, "Der neue Himmel und die neue Erde," in *Wort und Wahrheit* (January, 1964), pp. 263–279.

vidual can and should refer to himself. An immersion into the flow of generations shows us Christ's salvific act even in a greater light: it is freed from narrow individualism that so easily leads to pietistic attitudes and broadens into a vision of the Christ of mankind, the Christ of the Cosmos. The individual is saved through the salvation of mankind and attains his share of the fruits of salvation through his participation in the human community.

f) A parish is made up of people of every age-level. Each individual expects the priest to help him interpret his more or less conscious life-situation, so that he can become more receptive for the truths of faith, the realization of which is preconditioned by the specific age-level. In so far as the pastor sees the parallel between human development and the growth of the life of faith, he will be able to avoid making inopportune demands on children and adolescents, and the correlation between truths of faith and the different age-levels will be a conscious part of his proclamation. Such pastoral care in accordance with human nature is the concrete application of Theodor Müncker's profound observation: "The unfolding of the self is the ontic ground of the unfolding of Christ."

CHAPTER XII

The Sinner

1.

WHILE THE EXPERIENCE of guilt needs to be interpreted from an anthropological point of view, the experience of sin can be clarified only from the viewpoint of Revelation. Sin is guilt carried before the face of God. God's opinion of and reaction to sin can be detected from the life of Jesus, who took upon Himself the sins of the world and thus drew God's anger onto Himself. His agony in the Garden (Luke, 22:44) gives a presentiment of God's direct reaction to sin. The agony of the otherwise fearless Jesus was certainly not merely His presentiment of the suffering that would follow. To confront God, loaded with sins, and to draw down His judgment on Himself makes Jesus "feel dread and to be exceedingly troubled" (Mark 14:33). What must sin be, if it causes this! What was open in the situation in the Garden of Gethsemane is closed to the sinner; he experiences, as could be said, only the outside of sin, the contradiction to the divine commandment. The catastrophe in his relationship to God is hidden. The sinner himself has no idea of his dangerous position.

This lack of awareness in the penitent is of real concern to

191

the priest who wishes to be of aid to the sinner. In order to be of help in an expert way he must study the "environment" of the mystery of sin. The change that takes place when one becomes a sinner is not the result of an accidental fall. Life's whole direction is frustrated, and all of the humanness of the individual participates in his changed life. An analysis of the sinner's development, his experience of sin and consequent experience of penitence, can give us an insight into both the sinner himself and the ways to help him. The parable of the prodigal son (Luke 15:11–31) and that of the weeds (Matt. 13:24–30) are the most valuable illustrations we can find.

2.

The parable of the prodigal son has two high points: the father's reception of his son and the conversion of the older brother. Both events are highlighted by the parable and constitute the kerygma. But the story is so full of actual life experiences that even the smaller details are of value for an understanding of the experience of the sinner.

It need not have been simply bad will that led the younger son to ask for his inheritance and to go out into the world. Perhaps he was even more talented than his brother who stayed at home and could even have left with the intention of finding a career in life and seeking mature responsibilities that would make his father proud of him later on. And possibly, his own inner vitality motivated him to face the dangers. The unknown is only an empty phrase until one has actually experienced its terrors. Though at first his naivete and lack of experience led him into bad company, he most likely encountered many opportunities to change his course. The long time spent in squandering his entire inheritance certainly must have offered some moments of recollection, of self-discovery, whereby he might have had occasion to be honest with himself and to openly face his guilt with a spiritual decision. His was not a sudden falling into sin, for he had undergone a development that included spiritual decisions and predecisions.

After guilt had driven him into extreme external misery, all kinds of possibilities now parade before his eyes: to succumb to resignation and let everything go, to harden in pride, to curse his bad luck. Then came the slowly penetrating insight: "My way of thinking was wrong. I am not right. I am evil. I have sinned." The prodigal's opening up for the last possibility, his acceptance of it and his consequent decision, is not something to be taken for granted; there are those who prefer to cling to the other possibilities. No one but the sinner himself knows how he will decide; and even he himself does not know before he makes the decision. He could also be lost for ever. The risk is so closely connected with uncertainty that he simultaneously experiences the frightening mystery of the interplay of free decision and grace, as well as a newness, a beginning, the creative aspect of contrition. On his way home the prodigal is overwhelmed with the awareness of his unworthiness. "I am no longer worthy to be called thy son" (Luke 15:19). Pardon gives this unworthiness its proper proportions and transforms it into humility: man has experienced his limits. Once more the terror of uncertainty is felt in the trembling joy of the father's welcome: "This my son was dead, and has come to life again; he was lost, and is found" (Luke 15:24). Between the "being dead" and "coming to life again," between the "being lost" and "being found again," is a breathless moment during which the person outside can only prayerfully await the free, unpredictable decision, that is, another beginning and the first link of a new chain of cause and effect. To be lost and to be found: this is the abyss the person outside peers into during the event, and the one the sinner sees *after* his salvation. A moment—this "minimum" of time fused with a "maximum" of intensity—can be decisive for life or for death! What danger and jeopardy for human life in the salvation-situation! The beneficent fear that follows the danger overcome, the salvation and return, makes the feast of thanksgiving all the more joyful. Of course, those who through their lack of zest for life or through over-protection have never experienced such constructive terror may be quite resentful, even scandalized, at a joyful feast on such an occasion.

What will be the new relationship between father and son? What will be their conversation during the feast, and later on? Here the question is not so much the content of the son's report of external events, but rather his deeper understanding of life and the world. The wise father is happy with the maturing son; the son who has changed now admires the father's wisdom of life. The relationship between the two has strengthened; forgiveness creates a new union. They are united in secret understanding of the heights and depths of life, its dangers and the miracle of salvation. The acceptance of the limits of man, along with a new sense of appreciation of the home and of the values of the world that it provides, create the possibility of a new beginning.

This description of the development of the sinner has negative as well as positive aspects. But we must be prevented from falling into a false mystique of sin;[1] hence while it is true that sin *can* contribute to maturity, sin nevertheless is not necessary for maturing, or even the only way that man can become mature. Maturity attained through sin is highly paid for in the uncertainty of the return, the possibility of being lost. To be responsible for the loss of a single individual because of a wrong interpretation concerning sin must be an almost unbearable burden for the priest or educator.

However, our primary concern here is to see the reality of the sinner and to understand his development in order to help him with efficacious care and guidance. For the sinner is not to be condemned; he is not merely something to be angrily

---

[1] Cf. "Sündenmystik," in *Lexicon für Theologie und Kirche,* 9, col. 1184.

tossed aside like a coin, or a sheep pushed into the abyss. Christ took a stand in word and deed against the Jewish concept of the sinner; man in sin is an object of special care, of pastoral care. The divine salvific act will extend to the sinner, thus demanding not only an understanding of the sinner, but also a proximity to him; it is necessary to pursue him and to leave the other ninety-nine alone for a while. This involves in each case a proximity to the abyss of sin, which can be a source of scandal for those looking on. Here it is necessary to point out that care for a sinner must include the possibility that onlooking fellow Christians lack understanding, and that, like the "older brother," they either cannot or will not comprehend what goes on within the sinner and can thus be irritated and even scandalized by a priest or layman who is in the company of "publicans and sinners." Pastoral care for the sinner is therefore based on two reflections: help for the sinner and consideration for the environment.[2]

Conversation with the sinner during all phases of his development must also attempt to interpret his experience. He will refuse to respond to an entreaty to give up his sinful ways and to return, so long as there is no differentiation between sin itself and an experience that can be positively evaluated. "I cannot feel sorry for it, it was enjoyable"—in such and similar formulations he defends his situation. Although the sinner takes a right-angle turn off the right road, he cannot disregard his experience and simply make an about-face and retrace his errant way. His error brought him into relation with things of the world, for even a wrong way is nevertheless a way into the world. Thus his sin occurs among and with things of the world that are good in themselves. True, sin sheds a false light on his dealing with worldly things, but both his biased view and the positive elements of experience hidden therein demand an interpretation. To say it figura-

[2] See Chap. XIII in this book.

tively, the return to the right road cannot be an about-face that takes him back over the original road, but must be more or less a wide, gradual curve.

We deal here with two concepts, one static, the other dynamic. Sin in itself must be seen as static: *No* is the only answer that can be given. But the development of the sinner is dynamic, also in his return, and his experience demands an interpreting No *and* Yes. Evil is certainly called evil, but the positive and potentially positive must be clearly differentiated from it. Such pastoral care avoids breaking, burning and rejecting and tries instead to carefully bend, to warm and to guide. It is human guidance corresponding to God's way of thinking, as becomes clear in the sequence of Pentecost:

> Bend the stubborn heart and will
> Melt the frozen, warm the chill
> Guide the steps that go astray.

3.

The parable of the weeds (Matt. 13:24–30) has a valuable lesson for every form of human guidance: Whatever is positive in the experience of the sinner must be protected. This eschatological parable builds a bridge to the time of Christ's return and subjects the entire between-time to the law: "Let both grow together until the harvest" (Matt. 13:30). That which is not practicable in the farmer's field is also the rule of the field where good and evil grow—in mankind, in the Church, in the soul of the individual. Behind this surprising command is a precaution: "Lest in gathering the weeds you root up the wheat along with them" (Matt. 13:29). The wheat must be protected by all means; the good must not be damaged. It seems wiser to endure an intermingling of good and evil than to insist radically on separation and division. Rooting up the evil damages the good. Weeding is dangerous, not only because it is difficult to distinguish the weeds from the wheat (the sprouts of the bearded darnel look like wheat), but also because the roots of both are matted together. In the field where God's word is sown, the good is interspersed with the seed of evil. Our own disposition toward the sinner and care for the sinner should be in accordance with this attitude of Christ.

a) The drama of human sin is enacted on a stage behind a stage. The fact that the enemy is allowed to sow weeds presumably means that there is a hidden stage where God and Satan are the actors. Only a few scenes break through, like flashes of light, to the stage in the foreground. The first flash is a God-ordained enmity ("I will put enmity between you and the woman" [Gen. 3:15]); at the midpoint of the drama we glimpse Christ's death on the cross; and at the end Satan's final condemnation on the day of His return through the final revelation of the *mysterium iniquitatis* (Apoc. 20:7–10). Man is dragged into the action taking place in the background —on the stage behind the stage. But the fact is that he is only dragged into it. Thus, in spite of the terrible human drama of sin, the main accent is removed from the stage in the foreground, allowing the pastor to free himself from unbearable responsibility in his struggle against sin. His main concern should not be so much a fight against evil as a caring for what is good, even in the sinner. If in his parish the weeds spring up, his first concern should nonetheless be the protection of the good and the care for the good in the midst of the weeds. It is not his task to strive for a *pure* parish. Of course, this does not mean that he should close his eyes to reality; weeds must be called weeds, and the pastor is the one to point them out.

b) In the parable the lord expects his servants to allow

the weeds to grow—to watch sin grow, in spite of the wiles of the enemy, the clever camouflages and hidden temptations.[3] The risks the Lord takes upon Himself in this situation is a frightful mystery!

This attitude of the lord of the world finds a parallel in many life-situations. The physician expects the patient to endure the pain of an abscess until it is ripe. If he cuts too soon, the entire organism will be infected; if he cuts too late, the consequences are equally grave. Only experience can give the physician the courage to wait, to let the patient suffer until the inflammation has reached its peak; only then will he operate.

A similar phenomenon can be observed in education. Self-assertion, for instance, can be the expression of a strong personality—but also of pride. Only the dilettante is opposed to every urge for autonomy and independence. The words of Laotse tell us much regarding human nature and its guidance:

"That which one wishes to pull back must first extend; that which one wishes to weaken must first become strong; that which one wishes to conquer must first be allowed to fight."

Here again, only experience, courage and patient waiting can teach us the right moment to interfere. Especially in religious education this wisdom is often ignored. The result is a desert instead of a fertile field.

This patient wisdom is necessary also in politics even though it intensifies the risk. It takes more than courage and a healthy nervous system to sit back and watch the growth of a hostile organization, to see it grow in strength and in the clarity of its goals; to watch the opposition as it comes into existence, or the seeds of hostility growing in a foreign power. No statesman without confidence in his own experience and

[3] As a help in the "discernment of spirits," we recommend C. S. Lewis' *Screwtape Letters* (New York, 1943).

authority will for any length of time be able to play this game of rise and fall, of peace and war, of success and failure.

Yet God stands by and watches sin as it grows; He does not immediately interfere even when it is a matter of the salvation or damnation of the world and of the individual. How great His omnipotence if He can wait until the time of harvest before He interferes. The Lord expects this attitude also from His servants. Pastoral *activity* against sin and the sinner has its limits and should change into *passivity,* if it reaches the point where it is no longer a matter of warning, distinguishing and entreating, but rather a holy anger that drives one to tear things apart, throw them away, get people out of the parish, excommunicate them from the Church. Human attitudes see this as the way to protect the good, but the Lord forbids man to make a final judgment and orders him to wait until the harvest—this, He says, is His way to protect the good.

When people in the parish become indiscrete and publicize this "twilight" attitude of the pastor, he faces a new problem: "the older brother," or, as St. Paul formulates it, the consideration of the "weak." Co-ordinated to the protection of the good is the protection of the "weak."

CHAPTER XIII

The Mature and the Immature

1.

THE MAIN OBJECTION of those actively involved in pastoral care and education is that theorists demand too much of people. They maintain that people are not mature; that an innovation can be introduced but not maintained; that people are not independent in religious matters; that all are not capable of behavior possible only for the mature; that demands arc made on them as though they were a group of elite, while the majority of people, even in the Church, simply need to be guided, directed and led; that overdemand does not serve the life of faith, but rather irritates, aggravates and scandalizes people. Here we have the phenomenon of religious scandal as it can show up in all realms of pastoral care and education. In the realm of attitudes toward sinners, this scandal is typically represented in the New Testament by the "older brother."

The older brother is angry, irritated, aggravated; he deems it a scandal that his younger brother is given such a reception. Yet not the sinner, but he who had stayed at home is reprimanded by the father, who, of course, in the parable represents God. What are the reasons for his lack of understanding?

When we first glance at this over-all picture of life, we might easily think of the son who stayed home as a good, well-behaved child of the father; yet, compared with his younger brother he could have had a calmer disposition with little desire for change. His reproach to the father indicates as much: "Thou hast never given me a kid that I might make merry with my friends." Why did he himself not take the initiative to ask his father? This kind father certainly would have complied with it. The older son remained at home, was protected, always well behaved ("I have never transgressed one of thy commands" [Luke 15:29]). He knows nothing of the risk and temptation of one who is on his own; he has no idea of what goes on in a sinner and sees only superficially the bad intention, the failure and the loss of the inheritance. He has never realized the creatureliness of his own person and knows nothing about his own need of salvation. He is narrow, hard, self-righteous and always correct. Admittedly, he likewise had good intentions (as had the younger son when he left), but he is in danger of not understanding the father-God who gave such a kind welcome to his lost brother.

Such "older sons" we find in all areas of human life, for preservation from the danger of sin does not quite preserve one from a possible opposition to God. Correct moral behavior is no proof for a being-right before the God of Revelation. As in every form of human guidance, pastoral care, too, faces here the problem of the relationship between the mature and the immature, between adults and minors, the broadminded and the narrowminded, the *personal* and the pre*personal,* or, to be in line with St. Paul, between the "strong" and the "weak."

The Church at all times has considered pastoral care of the weak a matter of the heart and one of primary concern. Understanding her way of thinking and acting means to gain insight into her centuries-old wisdom in human guidance. These profound principles, formulated in modern terms, should be brought to the awareness of and made available to pastoral care. The concern here is not protection of the sinner, but protection of the weak. Thus, the strong confront the weak; their mutual relationship is to be learned from Holy Scripture.

2.

St. Paul approached this problem by considering a specific situation, namely, the "eating of meat" (Rom. 14:1–23; 15:1–2; I Cor. 8:1–13; 10:23–30). In his time buying at the meatmarket always included the risk of buying "ritualized" meat since there was hardly any meat that was not subjected to some pagan ritual.[1] The Christians reacted to this situation in various ways.

The "strong" ones knew that there is only one God, and no idols; hence they concluded that the religious rites had no power to infect the meat. Naturally it required courage and strength to free themselves from the customary way of thinking; but the consequence was knowing, recognition, "gnosis." St. Paul completely supports these "strong" people and their knowledge: "All things indeed are clean" (Rom. 14:20); "All things are lawful" (I Cor. 10:23); "Anything that is sold in the market, eat, asking no question for conscience' sake" (I Cor. 10:25–26); "If one of the unbelievers invites you, and you wish to go, eat whatever is set before you, and ask no question for conscience' sake" (I Cor. 10:27). "But such knowledge is not in everyone" (I Cor. 8:7). For this reason the *weak* are "meatless." They cannot free themselves from the customary thinking that forbids all contact with pagan cult, no matter how insignificant. True, they know that there is only one God who, through Christ's Epiphany, had freed all pagan cults from magic, but they have not the courage

---

[1] Cf. Otto Kuss, "Römerbriefkommentar," in *Regensburger Neues Testament* (Regensburg, 1940), VI, 101 ff.

to realize this knowledge in fruitful recognition, or to ignore a taboo and to free themselves from a past that has to be overcome. St. Paul very consciously calls "weak" those who cannot digest solid food and thus have to be fed with milk (I Cor. 3:2). But he never refers to the weak without at the same time advocating their protection. This responsibility, however, he throws upon the shoulders of the strong: "But him who is weak in faith, receive, without disputes about opinions" (Rom. 14:1). One should not despise him, nor judge him: "Let us not judge one another" (Rom. 14:13). "We, the strong, ought to bear the infirmities of the weak" (Rom. 15:1).

The problem here is not one of simple ignorance that teaching could dispel, but it is something more difficult, something deeper, beyond the reach of reproaches, and not a simple question of guilt. What is needed is a maturing in faith, which is a combination of grace and one's own effort, and which therefore must be respected. Thus it is unfair to look down on the simple people. Whoever takes this attitude—and this is the first admonition to the strong—"has not yet known as he ought to know" (I Cor. 8:2). He is like a physician who treats people without consideration for their pain and, therefore, frightens many away. A mode of thinking that makes one feel superior to others, taking pleasure in itself (Rom. 15:2), not really knowing (I Cor. 8:2) and puffed up (I Cor. 8:1), ignores the fact that there are many and various painful ways leading from a "knowledge of the head" to a "knowledge of the heart." But true understanding knows more, not only truth but also the effect of truth, that truth is hard to gain and even harder to realize. For truth must be united with love, only then does it "edify" (I Cor. 8:1) faith and maturity. The "strong" are those who know this, who have insight and who thus can understand and guide the weak. Knowledge obliges.

The second admonition to the strong explains why the weak need protection. Whoever demands that the weak eat "pagan" meat, might "wound their weak conscience" (I Cor. 8:12); for very likely they will eat in spite of their doubts, in spite of their being scandalized (Rom. 14:20), and with hesitation (Rom. 14:23). He would then be doing something that "is not from faith" (Rom. 14:23). And "this right of yours" (of the strong) would then become a "stumbling block to the weak" (I Cor. 8:9)—"through thy 'knowledge' the weak one will perish" (I Cor. 8:11).

They are weak because they cannot free themselves from traditions; they depend too much on external opinions; they do not stand within themselves; they live pre*personally,* for their *person* is not actuated. They are immature, undeveloped and, therefore, insecure in so far as God is concerned; their conscience is not sure of itself. Their relationship with God needs a shelter that protects it from the storm and the cold. A sudden imposition would interfere with the conditions of growth in their relationship with God. The strong should know that trying to force someone into religious maturity can have the opposite effect and cause a violent reaction of his nature. Whoever, for instance, confronts a child with a situation requiring insight, goes too far; whoever demands a *personal* attitude from one who is still living pre*personally,* irritates him and arouses feelings of resentment; whoever burdens the weak with the freedom of the Gospel—with the "knowledge" of Paul—makes demands that the weak cannot fulfill in their religious life; the weak misinterpret this "knowledge" and even feel that it is antireligious. But since they are taught this by brothers of their own faith they are either scandalized or may consent to eat with a bad conscience.

Enforced maturity causes violence to one's relationship with God and thus damages it. Christ died also for the weak (Rom. 14:15; I Cor. 8:11). "To his own lord he stands or falls; but he will stand, for God is able to make him stand" (Rom 14:4). Something happens between the weak and God that allows them to come to salvation—"makes them stand," something that escapes our human way of thinking—but it must not be disturbed by scandal. "Do not for the sake of food destroy the work of God" (Rom. 14:20). This is the third admonition to the strong: Christ Himself stands protectingly over the weak.

St. Paul then comes to one's actual behavior at a meal where the weak are present. If the weak should be scandalized by the eating of meat, the strong should take this into consideration and should also refrain from eating meat. "Therefore, if food scandalizes my brother, I will eat flesh no more forever" (I Cor. 8:13). St. Paul goes on now to extend this thought into other areas: "It is good not to eat meat and not to drink wine, nor to do anything by which thy brother is offended or scandalized or weakened" (Rom. 14:21). In the company of the weak the degree of their maturity must be taken into consideration. All this is a one-sided obligation on the part of the strong, but their position is also strengthened. St. Paul not only stands firm on their behalf, but also offers them two suggestions that enable them to practice a sincere consideration of others. He says that the strong one, the free, mature and adult one, shall hold fast to the knowledge he has gained: "Keep the conviction you have before God" (Rom. 14:22). Hence, he is not to become insecure, even though he is alone or with a mere few or confronted with a whole multitude. Paul, therefore, protects the conscience of the strong; for the stilted conscience of the weak is by no means a yardstick. The freedom of the strong is never to be judged by another's conscience (I Cor. 10:29). One should even refuse to be ill spoken of and insulted because of this freedom (Rom. 14:16; I Cor. 10:30), and thus, when among certain people, it is better not to talk about it at all.

The endorsement that St. Paul gives to the mature recognizes that the state of freedom is a gift of the spirit of God, even though this grace does not replace that which can be attained only by man's own striving for maturity. This recognition makes it possible to deal with the weak, not with false pity, but in true solidarity, so that their human dignity is preserved and no injustice is done to God's beloved, simple people, but that, on the contrary, they will be helped. Christ's allusion to the flock without a shepherd is directed to the immature who lack orientation and who need guidance, and also to the mature to whom, together with the blessing of freedom, the responsibility for the immature is given. From this, pastoral care, education and guidance of the soul must draw their consequences.

3.

The Gospel calls upon the strong, yet reports many occasions of Christ's tenderness toward the weak. Christ says, for instance, "Anyone who so much as looks with lust at a woman has already committed adultery with her in his heart" (Matt. 5:28). This invites keen, constant awareness, that is, *personal* alertness. But when He is confronted with an adultress, he calls the sin a sin: "*Sin* no more" (John 8:11), yet protects the woman who sinned. Pastoral care and education must combine both poles in order to help people and to be able to carry out the command of the Gospel.

a) The parish sociological structure is in the shape of a pyramid, educationally as well as economically. But it is also a pyramid of the strong and the weak, of mature and immature, of those living *personally* and those pre*personally,* which is more important for the pastor since these structures are directly co-ordinated to the Gospel. Pastoral-sociological surveys of other structures are merely of secondary importance, as they do not reach the core of the relationship between Creator and creature, Christ and man, Gospel and the person, God's call and human response. The *personal* view with all its variations, ranging from the freedom of the actualized person to the unfreedom of the pre*personal,* cuts across all sociological considerations. There are the "strong" among the lower classes, just as there are "weak" ones among the highest social levels. Thus pastoral care can become quite complicated for the simple reason that the mature and the "strong" are to be found among the simple folk who have had only a minimum of formal education and, at the same time, the religiously immature and the "weak" ones among the educated. Thus if the proclamation would be directed only to the educated, perhaps because a parish might have a majority of highly educated people, the concern of the Gospel would never be met. Proclamation speaks to man, reaches to man's core and has the character of a personal call; the intelligence and education of the hearers play only a secondary role in the true proclamation. The purpose of proclamation is not to promote education, but to confront the human person with the divine Person. The success of pastoral care is dependent upon the degree of the actualization of the person. The more a pastor clearly understands this in a living association with his parishioners, the more he can adjust general principles to individual needs.

Pastoral care must do justice to both the weak and the strong. It must avoid making excessive demands on those who live pre*personally* and, at the same time, offer spiritual nourishment to the faith life of those living *personally*. Pastoral care that is biased and exclusively *personal* cannot be digested by most people; they will react negatively and perhaps stay away. Young, overzealous priests, and even certain Protestant religions, have a dangerous tendency toward overstressing the *personal*. On the other hand, however, completely pre*personal* pastoral care suiting the needs of simple souls is the temptation for priests who are veterans in the field. They base their arguments on their own successes and on the experience of the centuries. This is an attitude not at all uncommon in the Catholic Church today. Pre*personal* pastoral care, however, is no longer sufficient for modern man, since he no longer tends to hide behind a muted pulpit-Catholicism, in awe of the preacher, but rather more and more "individuals" are steadily seeking and finding their way to *personal* actualization. Thus pastoral care must combine both approaches.

Such bipolar pastoral care (and this holds true also for education and all human guidance) in proclamation, instruction and guidance of souls presents a problem of language, of methods as well as the *personal* state of development of the pastor.

b) Parishioners gathered together in church represent a cosmos of all ages, social levels and educational backgrounds, also of all the various levels of human maturity. To address them all at the same time and yet to bring home to each one the message of the Sunday is possible only because the content of the Gospel refers not to intellectual concepts but to universally human experiences that, when given life by the preacher, equally fascinate the simple and differentiated individual as well.[2] As we know, the Gospel is neither a theory nor a philosophy; but it is a message. It is the Revelation of God directed to man, understandable by all men. Thus the language should be universally human both from the viewpoint of the Revelation and from that of its listeners. It should interpret human experience, put human life into words and be molded by universally human, typical situations of life. Naturally this implies that the speaker has not only differentiated his own humanness, but that he is also aware of it so as to establish a full relationship with the world.

The extent that the language of the Gospel is co-ordinated to reality becomes evident when placing the homily in the dimension of time. In so far as it is a report of God's salvific deeds of the past, the proclamation is *memoria,* the memory of Christ. But the homily is also intended to manifest the

---

[2] Cf. Josef Goldbrunner's essay "Urbilder—Schlüsselbegriffe—Archetypen" in *Katechetische Blätter* (January, 1964), pp. 1–6.

symbolic character of God's salvific acts in view of the *prophetia,* the prophecy of Christ. Thus proclamation in liturgy reveals the hidden presence of both the past and the future through the celebration of the mysteries of salvation, and here it is *mysterium,* the mystery of Christ. The activation of the elements of the present salvation-situation[3] means not only to stimulate intellectual reflections but, since these elements are realities, also to create the possibility of their realization.

It is true that some are satisfied with the accounts of holy deeds, and the *memoria* would be sufficient for them. But this is no reason to limit the homily to an interesting description of what has happened (even though, as in a seed, everything present and future is contained therein). One should never forget that God's grace and man's openness to it may allow him to experience at least presentiments of the Gospel through the *prophetia* and the *mysterium.* But one thing is certain, that the Christian life of those who have made progress in *personal* actualization cannot sustain itself with mere *memoria* but must nourish itself with the *prophetia* and the *mysterium.*

c) The methods of pastoral care are determined not only by the task of transmitting the personal call of the Gospel, but also by the capability of those called to live either on the *personal* or on the pre*personal* level. *Personal* methods are directly in accord with the Gospel and, therefore, should outweigh the pre*personal* auxiliary methods, since the purpose of the latter is to provide opportunities for the pre*personal* to become open for the *personal.*

The keyword for the *personal* approach in Christian pastoral care is "invitation" (Matt. 22:2–10). To invite out of free good will—this is the first element; the freedom to accept or reject the invitation calls for a decision—this is the second element. Thus the one who invites gives himself partly into

---

[3] Cf. above, p. 6. The fourth element, pain, deserves a book in itself since it is the most frequent theme in pastoral care.

the hands of the other; this is a weakness—the third element of all *personal* categories. The *personal* approach is generally at a loss when confronted with great crowds of people. How very possible to make a fool of oneself in trying such an approach! And yet, only the *personal* categories are worthy of the dignity of man and of the Gospel. A listing of some of the *personal* categories shows how the three elements mentioned above can be found in whole or in part in each of them: inviting, wooing, asking, admonishing, forgiving, thanking, praising, loving. Common to all these categories, for example, is the fact that their intensity can increase and decrease. To the extent such invitations, expressions of thanks, of love and of forgiveness are repeated, that much more is their intensity felt. But it is not possible to count them, or even to weigh them, that is, to make a pre*personal* evaluation of them. Thus we come to the fourth element of *personal* categories—they are related, as is divine grace, to quality, not to quantity.

The very fact that in the actual practice of the Christian life quantitative thinking is so widespread and has such a firm hold proves that pastoral care based on *personal* methods alone is much too demanding and thus must be combined with pre*personal* categories. Consequently, a vital concern of guidance and of pastoral care is to use pre*personal* methods to the degree they are needed, that is, without allowing quantitative religious tendencies to run rampant, but rather orientating them to the *personal*.

Those who cannot decide for themselves must be led, sometimes even forced. Thus the laziness and lassitude of the masses and their whimsical reactions to pleasure or displeasure have led the Church in her pastoral office to use pre*personal* methods similar to those of the Old Testament. The Church has had rigorous and brutal men like Elias, stern men of the law, intransigently intolerant, who have maintained that "the quiet whisper achieves nothing . . . a violent storm is necessary. . . . They have actually made nations bend under the power of this terror"—and made them surrender to the Church. These men of power addressed the Church: "If it were only a matter of the humble and the mild, your name would long have been forgotten among the nations. The great mass of men is led to right action only by iron force."[4] Such force can be put into practice by one or more of the following methods: Enforcing religion through political power, ruling society exclusively by tradition and social ostracism.

But methods of force no longer serve the Gospel in this era of the unfolding person, for they do not permit decision, but rather hinder individual maturing. Coercion is a block to the *personal;* it is not even pre*personal* but a*personal.* Thus the present situation requires that we clearly differentiate methods and allow only those that are at least open for the *personal* methods, which, while guiding the life of community, nevertheless do not hinder individual awakening. Even the pre*personal* methods, far from anything that approaches the coercive, should accompany a simultaneous call to the *personal.* The flock is surrounded by a fence but the shepherd himself opens the gate to the individuals who can manage their freedom.

Force must be replaced by organization.[5] A schedule of services, for instance, teaches the parish discipline and makes it aware of the necessity of becoming accustomed to regularity. A well-organized religion class with strict discipline provides a shelter for the child where he not only learns but also hears the "invitation." It prevents the child from creating disturbances. However, children in a religion class should never be humiliated because of their irreligious attitudes. Their presence in the class should be a welcome challenge to the mature teacher. It is also commendable to *invite* the entire class to

[4] Cf. Peter Lippert, "Moses and Elias Stand Beside Thee," in *Job the Man Speaks with God* (New York, 1936).

[5] Cf. Egon Colomb, "Seelsorgeplanung in der Grosstadt," in *Trierer Theologische Zeitschrift,* 72 (1963), 129–249.

regularly scheduled participation in sacramental life; but anyone who does not accept should not be punished or made to feel ashamed. Anxiety should be replaced by fear based on an authority that combines objectivity, dignity, human kindness, and secure guidance—an interplay of distance and closeness. Non-Christian religions are often based on anxiety before God; Christianity is grounded in fear. True authority does not instill fear but awakens reverence. While fear inhibits the powers of man, reverence stimulates the growth of independent strength. The authority of the pastor is a prism for the authority of God.

The difference between force and organization, between fear and reverence, shows how pre*personal* methods, in contradistinction to the a*personal,* are open to a *personal* awakening. Certain pre*personal* methods can further the development of organization and authority: intelligent administration of parish business (modern and efficient methods); social activity (through parish clubs, societies, mixers, meetings); large-scale experiences (parish processions, rallies, diocesan-wide demonstrations) and finally the persuasive power of a preacher.

Pre*personal* methods are an irreplaceable aid to pastoral care but are also a constant danger in their tendency to get out of hand and to repress *personal* methods. Pastoral care on this level is, of course, more convenient, and comfortable as well, since one can rest in the security that this type of care for centuries has provided past generations with doctrine and the means of grace and has molded them in a traditional piety familiar to everyone. Such security in the pre*personal* approach, however, can have dire consequences.

The historical fact that the Church could not assimilate the explosive break-through of the person during the Protestant Reformation is a posteriori proof that the energies of mankind push on to further personalization whenever the time (the Kairos, or the historical Logos) is ripe. A great rushing tide toward personalization seems to be gathering momentum today in the members of the Church, as a counter-movement, so to speak, to the even wider stream of leveling collectivization.

The forces that today strive for the break-through of the *personal* are no less strong than those of the time of the Reformation. If this time they are to be individuated and integrated by the Church, then a corresponding pastoral care running on a second track—a *personal* pastoral care parallel to the pre*personal*—is needed. What happened in the Second Vatican Council for the good of the Church as a whole, a channel through which the forces dammed up for so many years can at last flow, should be made available to the individual through *personal* pastoral care in the parish.

d) The pastor's attempts to become mature enough to ride both tracks at the same time can create an inner shock. His idealism clashes with reality. Insuperable traditions, unbending through the centuries, seem to make new adjustments impossible, yet to be obedient to them would mean denying the spirit of the times, living and acting against knowledge and nature. In this resistance he finds himself in a situation so fluid that it slips through his fingers when he tries to grasp it, and yet so solid that he rams his head into a wall. He can reach a point of dismay—whether anyone or anything can be trusted.

Yet this bipolarity of rebellion and resignation can cause a ripening of his understanding for both the inflexible and the flexible, for the weak and the strong, for the *personal* and the pre*personal*. To the extent that he has actualized his own person, he can now orientate the skepticism of the older generation and make cautious preparation for far-sighted changes. Between the demands of his task and his maturity rules the law of reciprocal effect. The tasks challenge him, and his maturity moves him to face the tasks more profoundly and to fulfill them more expertly.

For instance, perhaps his proclamation of the Word of God has been a real success, and he becomes suddenly aware, to his own surprise, of having reached a new peak of human life. Yet he realizes that, no matter how much the sermon was the expression of his own individuality, the fruit of his own experience, it was "He" who spoke through him; he was only the medium, everything was "service"—the word was message. *Personal* life is the medium for transcending into the beyond. But this is simultaneously a confirmation and limitation of one's own being, its elevation and subordination. Human, individual being is accepted and becomes permeable for the divine Being. The actualization of the person is the apex of being-a-human and through it is effected the realization of the Christian.

The pastor who becomes a more and more actualized person may experience various reactions in his parishioners. On the one hand, they may become depressed, irritated, shaken, insecure, as if every feeling of resentment is being aroused in unconscious defense. Even the greatest reserve and objectivity, friendliness and helpfulness, cannot change these reactions. But, on the other hand, it could easily be that the *personal* life already existent below the surface hears the call and dares to come forth. In both instances it is a matter of the resonance of the person to *personal* life, expressing itself either in an intensified urge to escape or in the courage to take hold of one's existence. Person is resonant to *person*.

Possibly, the pastor who has reached such a degree of Christian realization may meet a wall of unconscious defense that isolates him from his parish. "Person is the greatest loneliness," says Bonaventure.[6] But we must add immediately that suddenly *personal* life breaks through in several individuals—often the pastor has paid for it with painful sacrifice. In all

---

[6] " . . . ad personalitatem requiritur ultima solitudo" (John Dun Scotus, Ox. II, d.1. q. 1.1. 17).

these experiences the pastor will find invaluable help in friendships with other priests and with mature lay people—the latter, however, outside the realm of pastoral activity. For pastoral effectiveness demands not only closeness but also distance; here, too, it participates in the life of the great messenger of God, His own Son.

Index

217